AVOIDING THE PITFALLS OF STARTING YOUR OWN BUSINESS

AUTHOR'S PREVIOUS BOOKS

Marketing on a Shoestring

The Achievement Challenge: How to be a "10" in Business
(with Don Beveridge)

Getting New Clients, *(with Richard A. Connor, Jr.)*

Marketing to the Fortune 500

Blow Your Own Horn: How to Market Yourself and Your
Career

Marketing Your Community

Checklist Management: The Eight-Hour Manager

Marketing Your Consulting and Professional Services

AVOIDING THE PITFALLS OF STARTING YOUR OWN BUSINESS

Jeffrey P. Davidson, C.M.C., M.B.A.

WALKER AND COMPANY
New York

To Judy,

*Silently the memory of you roams within
the inner reaches of my mind.
Fear not; I will carry you with me for the
rest of my life.*

First published in the United States of America
in 1988 by the Walker Publishing Company, Inc.

Published simultaneously in Canada by Thomas Allen & Son
Canada, Limited, Markham, Ontario.

Library of Congress Cataloging-in-Publication Data

Davidson, Jeffrey P.
  Avoiding the Pitfalls of Starting Your Own Business
     p. cm.
  Bibliography: p.
  Includes index.
  ISBN 0-8027-1012-3
  1. New business enterprises—United States—Management. 2. Small
business—United States—Management. I. Title.
HD62.5.D38 1988   87-23274
658.4'2—dc19   CIP

Printed in the United States of America
10 9 8 7 6 5 4 3 2

Contents

Introduction   1

CHAPTER 1
The Entrepreneurial Decade   5

CHAPTER 2
A Closer Look At Business Failure   16

CHAPTER 3
Are You Entrepreneurial Material?   27

CHAPTER 4
The Business Plan Monster   35

CHAPTER 5
Management Misconceptions   61

CHAPTER 6
The Financing Blues   77

v

110606

CONTENTS

CHAPTER 7
Personnel Problems   95

CHAPTER 8
Cost and Operation Control   115

CHAPTER 9
Computer System Foul-ups 101   128

CHAPTER 10
A Matter of Location   138

CHAPTER 11
Passing the Collection Plate   153

CHAPTER 12
Pitfalls with Professional Help   166

CHAPTER 13
Marketing Mania   179

CHAPTER 14
For Contractors Only   191

CHAPTER 15
Reentering the Corporate World   205

Glossary   217

Bibliography   227

Small Business Administration District Offices   229

Service Corps of Retired Executives (Score) Chapter Locations   232

Index   237

List of Charts,
Exhibits

Failure Trend Index   9

"Causes" of Failure   19

Business Failure Index by Industry   20

Business Failure Index by State   23

Business Plan Outline   38

SBA Business Plan and Qualifications Résumé   46

Records-Retention Timetable   68

12-Month Cashflow Projection Form   85

Break-even Computations   117

Traditional Control Procedures   124

What the Computer Advertisements Promise Versus
Reality   132

Neighborhood Shopping Center   140

Collection Difficulties Over Time   155

Further Reading on Marketing and Marketing Plans   184

Good Books on Selling   186

Reentering the Corporate World—A Graphic Portrayal   209

I would like to acknowledge Katherine J. Reynolds, Dianne L. Walbrecker, and Louis P. Baron for their editorial assistance and helpful input. Robert Bird and Jeanne Wolfe helped proofread portions of the manuscript. Brenda Earner and Sandy Stiner helped with the galleys. Judy Dubler offered her usual excellent word processing support.

AVOIDING THE PITFALLS OF STARTING YOUR OWN BUSINESS

Introduction

This is not a "how-to" book. There are currently hundreds of books available on how to start and manage your own business. Rather, you are about to read a "here's what" book. It conveys my experience and observations regarding what you need to know to make an informed decision as to whether or not you should start your own venture.

In many respects, this book is more valuable to would-be entrepreneurs than, and should be read before, books on how to start your own business. The complexities of operating your own business have increased to the point where this book becomes a necessity. If you don't know what you are getting into—the broad range of problems, heartaches, and potential catastrophic losses, then you are gambling with very high stakes—your career and your personal net worth.

1

Despite the grim statistics on failures of new business, each new entrepreneur believes that he/she can avoid the pitfalls that drive the majority of small businesses over the brink. Based on my experience as a management consultant—working with over 225 entrepreneurs since 1975—I have laid out for you high probability scenarios that you will be likely to face.

Would our nation's divorce rate be at 50 percent if all those contemplating marriage took the time to seriously consider, study, and assess what they were getting into? Probably not. Yet those in a high emotional state, such as being in love, are not likely to want to read a sober discussion of the difficulties of maintaining a stable marriage.

A HIGHLY EMOTIONAL STATE

And so it is with entrepreneurism. Those seeking to start their own ventures are in a highly emotional state. The natural inclination is to proceed full speed ahead and not worry about what so often happens to "the other guy." However, if you are seeking to start a business, or if you have been in business for a while, your probability of becoming "the other guy"—failing in your business—is extraordinarily high.

The psychic income of being your own boss often becomes poor compensation for the loss in real dollar income that most entrepreneurs will suffer in their early years. Being your own boss means that a tremendous amount of time must be spent on a never-ending variety of duties. This book will convey to you the magnitude and complexities of the various hazards you will encounter—in the prebusiness phase, during start-up, and for the first few years thereafter.

This book is for both the first-time entrepreneurs and those who have already "gotten their feet wet." In my prebusiness workshops, I have consistently found that 50 percent or more of any group has already been in business for a year or two before deciding to produce a business plan, seek outside financial assistance, and/or take on a management consultant. Vast numbers of new entrepreneurs rush in headlong, blithely bypassing crucial planning and preparation stages.

Life is a risk, and starting your own business is a compounded risk. Failing to comprehend the magnitude and nature of the risk is not in your best interest. Proceeding on target, with your eyes open, is. If you've recently entered the entrepreneurial arena, or are contemplating the plunge, then what follows pertains specifically to you.

Chapter 1, The Entrepreneurial Decade, will review the play entrepreneurism has received from the media against the backdrop of an ever-increasing number of small business failures. Chapter 2, A Close Look at Business Failure, examines how failed entrepreneurs did themselves in. It also examines failures by particular industry and by geography.

In Chapter 3, Are You Entrepreneurial Material?, basic skills, attitudes, and traits of entrepreneurs are presented to aid in your self assessment of whether you have what it takes. Chapter 4, The Business Plan Monster, presents the outline for the traditional business plan with commentary on the awesome task of completing selected components of the plan. Logically, one would assume that all sound businesses start with a sound business plan. Based on my experience, however, the majority of entrepreneurs still manage to ignore this crucial step.

In Chapter 5, Management Misconceptions, we'll discuss some of the myths of being your own boss and examine the formidable amount of paperwork and red tape you will continuously encounter. In Chapter 6, The Financing Blues, we'll explore why preparation for outside financing must start far in advance of the actual need, why cultivation of professional relations with loan officers is essential, and how the appearance of desperation is detrimental to the quest for financial assistance. We'll discuss the necessity for producing a cash flow, for strengthening your credit rating and what you are likely to encounter when seeking second-round financing.

In Chapter 7, Personnel Problems, we'll take a wide angle view of a variety of employee/management–related problems including hiring, productivity, absenteeism, and other challenges. In Chapter 8, Cost and Operation Control, the high cost of payroll, cost of goods sold, energy, and marketing will be discussed. Chapter 9, Computer System Foul-ups 101, makes this point: A computer system can probably be a great asset in your business, but to be truly effective, it will take weeks if not months of painstaking supervision and training.

Chapter 10, A Matter of Location, discusses the dilemmas of finding "the right spot" that plague first-time entrepreneurs. In Chapter 11, Passing the Collection Plate, a number of horror stories illustrate how collections can threaten the survival of almost every new enterprise.

Chapter 12 is entitled Pitfalls with Professional Help. While the most prevalent problem in this area is not seeking professional help, there are many things that can and will go wrong when you work with outside professionals. Chapter 13, Marketing Mania, explores such insidious traps as diving in without looking, trying to be all things to all customers, and not allocating enough resources to marketing.

Chapter 14 is entitled For Contractors Only. This chapter specifically focuses on problems contractors face in the areas of bidding, customer expectations, and revenue forecasting. Many of the principles involved are relevant to all entrepreneurs.

The final chapter in the book, Chapter 15, Reentering the Corporate World, discusses the loneliness of the entrepreneurial life, the opportunity costs of having been away and the readjustment problems of entrepreneurs who seek to make their way back to the corporate world.

Being in business for yourself represents a supreme challenge, and if recognized as such, can be a profitable, rewarding experience. However, in order to reach that hallowed ground, you'll probably have to invest more time, more energy, and more of your personal and financial resources than you ever dreamed would be required to be successful. If you are determined to become an entrepreneur, reading this book is an excellent first step.

CHAPTER 1

The Entrepreneurial Decade

The reasonable man adapts himself to the world, the unreasonable man attempts to adapt the world to himself. Therefore all progress depends on the unreasonable man.

—GEORGE BERNARD SHAW

The 1980s by many counts will be remembered as the decade of the entrepreneur. Entrepreneurs and "entrepreneurial types" within larger corporations consistently shared the celebrity spotlight, gracing the covers of such publications as *Time, Parade, Newsweek,* and other popular nonbusiness magazines. Exploits of T. Boone Pickens, Steven Jobs, Debbi Fields, and numerous others have been recorded, filmed, rerecorded, and canonized.

After years of cautiously circling and misunderstanding, the business entrepreneur and the journalist finally got to know one another. In most cases they liked what they saw. The dramatic growth of *Inc., Venture, D&B Reports, Entrepreneur,* and a host of other magazines geared specifically to the entrepreneur fed the widespread obsession with operating your own business.

From the highest levels of the federal government to college and high school classrooms, the virtues of entrepreneurism have been widely extolled.

Ted Turner, Peter Ueberroth, Malcolm S. Forbes, Donald Trump, and H. Ross Perot among others are basking in the media limelight. The last time entrepreneurs were so celebrated throughout the land was in the roaring 1920s, just before the Great Depression.

The ultrasuccessful entrepreneur of today is put on a pedestal alongside athletes, entertainers, politicians, the gifted, and the beautiful. Although the average would-be small business entrepreneur is focusing more on making a healthy living than getting on the cover of *Time*, the current entrepreneurial craze still is fueled in good part by those entrepreneurs who have become media darlings.

In some way, perhaps subliminally, John Q. Citizen gets the notion that the entrepreneurial life is just what he has been waiting for and will provide the rewards he has been seeking.

Not one sentence in a recent *Business Week* cover story entitled "Business Celebrities" focused on the extraordinary numbers who tried and failed to be like those written about. All the world loves a winner, but there just are not that many of them.

What role do the popular business books play in propagating the myths of entrepreneurship? Walk into any B. Dalton, Waldenbooks, or other chain or independent bookstore to the business book section. You will see fifteen to twenty titles on how to start, operate, and be successful in your own business.

A few of these books devote a chapter or perhaps a part of a chapter to the pitfalls of entrepreneurism and thus, in some measure, attempt to provide a balanced picture. If you are lucky, you might come across one or two books that provide a useful perspective on the cons as well as the pros of the entrepreneurial experience.

I believe that by focusing on the downside of entrepreneurship as well as the upside, one can gain the wisdom necessary to make an intelligent decision about starting on the entrepreneurial path.

A NEW ERA

New business start-ups have been averaging over 600,000 per year for the last several years. As we enter the 1990s, the rapid rate of new business start-ups could scarcely be expected to continue. Normal increases in the population foster new businesses to serve the continuing and new needs of more consumers. Yet, the rate of new business start-ups since 1980 far exceeds increases in population.

There are now fourteen million small businesses in the United States according to the U.S. Small Business Administration. Over three million businesses are owned by women—more than double the number in 1975.

In addition, there are now ten million independent entrepreneurs, as reported by the Department of Commerce. Many of these are not counted in the figures presented by the Small Business Administration. These independent entrepreneurs are often employed by someone else full-time and have launched their own businesses on the side. A large number are waiting for that moment when they can leave their full-time positions to devote one hundred percent of their time to their own ventures. Added to the above are several million who have never started a business but are contemplating doing so.

Courses and well-developed programs on launching a business venture are available through universities, adult education programs, the Small Business Administration, and private training firms. Many of those who take these courses never do launch a venture of their own. Still the number who are in "entrepreneurial training" continues to grow at a healthy rate.

BEHIND THE SPLASHY COVER STORY

Often in a media society, followup stories to those with splashy headlines are simply not written, or if they are, are buried some place inside the publication. The cold, cruel facts are that the failure rate has more than doubled in the last thirty years and more than tripled the relatively low failure rates of the 1970s. The failure rate in the 1980s exceeds all previous levels.

As social, technological, and economic changes take place in society, entrepreneurs face an array of new complexities that would test the mettle of even the most worthy soul. Perhaps there is no greater myth in society today than the notion that "operating your own business" is guaranteed to be a desirable, fulfilling goal.

We have all witnessed the grand opening or kickoff campaign of a new business that in a few short years—even months—went into painful bankruptcy. Still, we continue to fail to temper our view of entrepreneurism with any resemblance of reality.

7

D&B'S BUSINESS FAILURE INDEX

Since 1920, the Dun & Bradstreet Corporation has been the only significant and continuing source of information on small business failures. The D&B business failure index is a *relative* indicator, not an *absolute* number of business failures. It is based on the number of failures (according to D&B's limited definition of business failure) per 10,000 concerns listed in the D&B data base of 8,000,000 companies.

If the index is at 36, for example, such as in 1974, companies failed that year at a rate of 36 per 10,000 listed in the D&B data base. In 1984, for every 10,000 companies in the D&B sample data base, 107 failed (see chart next page).

Unfortunately, no concise, timely, national compilation of actual business failures is available. However, the D&B index is still a useful tool to examine the national trend. Also, unlike other, more limited resources, it can be used for interindustry or multiyear comparison.

On a weekly basis, D&B *Weekly Business Failures* lists the number of failures in its data base, the year to date total, and changes from previous periods. It also includes a thirteen-week moving average of failures plus comment and analysis.

On a monthly basis, D&B publishes *Monthly Business Failures*, which charts the number of failures and liabilities in its data base of over 100 lines of business. Data are broken down by liability size, major industry group, state, region, and selected cities. On a quarterly basis, D&B publishes the *Quarterly Business Failures Report*, which includes an index of failures and liabilities in its data base by detailed lines of business including data for two-digit, three-digit and most four-digit Standard Industrial Classification codes.

On an annual basis, D&B publishes the *Business Failure Record*, which offers an index of the numbers of failures and liabilities by state and region, by major industry group and by age of business. The *Record* also includes information on the reported causes of failure plus historical failure data.

Thousands of firms are started every week, many either fail or discontinue, and others transfer ownership or control. Each business day, D&B reports that over thirty-five thousand changes are made to their data base. New names are added while other names are deleted. Name styles are altered and financial information is updated. D&B sees this as evidence of the dynamic change and turnover constantly taking place in a business community.

D&B's FAILURE TRENDS INDEX

	Number of failures*	Total failure liabilities	Failure index
1956	12,686	$562,697,000	48
1957	13,739	615,293,000	52
1958	14,964	728,258,000	56
1959	14,053	692,808,000	52
1960	15,445	938,630,000	57
1961	17,075	1,090,123,000	64
1962	15,782	1,213,601,000	61
1963	14,374	1,352,593,000	56
1964	13,501	1,329,223,000	53
1965	13,514	1,321,666,000	53
1966	13,061	$1,385,659,000	52
1967	12,364	1,265,227,000	49
1968	9,636	940,996,000	39
1969	9,154	1,142,113,000	37
1970	10,748	1,887,754,000	44
1971	10,326	1,916,929,000	42
1972	9,566	2,000,244,000	38
1973	9,345	2,298,606,000	36
1974	9,915	3,053,137,000	38
1975	11,432	4,380,170,000	43
1976	9,628	$3,011,271,000	35
1977	7,919	3,095,317,000	28
1978	6,619	2,656,006,000	24
1979	7,564	2,667,362,000	28
1980	11,742	4,635,080,000	42
1981	16,794	6,955,180,000	61
1982	24,908	15,610,792,000	88
1983	31,334	16,072,860,000	110
1984	52,078	29,268,646,871	107
1985p	57,067	33,375,867,961	114

The Dun & Bradstreet Corporation © 1985
Reprinted with permission
*in D&B *sample* data base

A CHILLING PARALLEL

The use of D&B's failure index helps to minimize differences when observing small business performance in the economy over the course of years. The current level of small business failures, based on the D&B index, is unprecedented in the last fifty years and shows no sign of tapering off. In 1980, when the D&B business failure index jumped from 28 to 42, there was no apparent cause for alarm. In 1981, when the figure jumped to 61, followed by 81 in 1982, there was sufficient reason to take note.

Something was clearly going wrong on a national level when, in 1983, the index rose to 110. The 110 figure exceeded each of the four years, beginning with 1926, prior to the Great Depression. In 1930, 1931, and 1932 the failure index ranged between 122 and 154—levels that were about to be exceeded in the late 1980s.

The high level of entrepreneurial activity was spurred by the strong economic recovery starting in 1983. The large number of start-ups will significantly impact the number of businesses that will fail in the next five to seven years.

IT'S WORSE THAN THE RECORD SHOWS

As mentioned, the D&B definition of business failure is not broad in scope. The D&B business failure statistics *do* include businesses that ceased operations following assignment or bankruptcy, ceased operations with losses to creditors after such actions as foreclosure or attachment, voluntarily withdrew leaving unpaid debts, voluntarily compromised with creditors, or were involved in court actions such as receivership, reorganization, or arrangement.

Also, D&B uses the term "new business start-up" as a more significant measure of the actual number of new businesses, since new incorporations could include many entities established principally for legal or tax purposes. Thus, the term new business start-ups refers to those activities in which a product or service is offered for profit to customers or clients. Hence, the D&B small business failure record *does not* represent, by any stretch of the imagination, total business closings. For example, businesses that discontinue operations for reasons such as loss of capital, inadequate profits, ill health of the entrepreneur, retirement, etc., are not part of the tabulations. If creditors are paid in full, even if the business ceases to operate, it is not counted by Dun & Bradstreet.

The alarming news about all this is that hundreds of thousands of businesses that continue in a state of lingering death are simply not counted. They manage to pay their bills and somehow stay afloat while essentially making the entrepreneur a slave to creditors and suppliers, consuming his/her life. Also, those businesses that devour an entrepreneur's life savings, force him/her to sell or remortgage the home, and are otherwise not healthy but still manage to honor all liabilities are not counted by D & B.

Notably missing from the D&B statistics are the large number of one-person service firms. Moreover, the total number of establishments tabulated by Dun & Bradstreet for selected industries is significantly less than the total number of establishments as presented in census publications.

For example, the SBA's and the Department of Commerce's Bureau of the Census data bases represent approximately fourteen million small businesses throughout the United States. The D&B data base contains information on approximately eight million businesses. Of the six million businesses not included in the D&B data base, the vast majority are smaller, have fewer assets, and even lower long-term chances for success. Hence, D&B's published index on business failures may be far less than the actual rate at which small businesses fail.

While the published information indicates that four out of five small businesses fail, the unpublished reality may well be that nine out of ten, or nineteen out of twenty actually fail, thus raising the inordinate risk of entrepreneurship and the true rate of failure to the epidemic level.

A DEARTH OF INFORMATION

The failure index is so high and the loss is so catastrophic, yet the downside of entrepreneurism is scarcely known by those who have most at stake. In checking references on the topic of small business failures, I was amazed to discover how few books address this issue. Using the Library of Congress data base I was able to find only seventeen citations since 1980, eleven of which were obscure government-related studies.

Could it be that the great American success story simply refuses to mention that which doesn't fit? Everyone knows at least one would-be entrepreneur who has failed and probably failed miserably. Yet, the entrepreneur probably never revealed the magnitude of the failure. In a world where looking good and showing up well predominate, entrepreneurial failures are minimized or "forgotten" in everyday discussions.

REFUSING TO BELIEVE

When lecturing on marketing and management of a small business, I present the grim data to attendees. Invariably, someone asks me why I am trying to discourage the group.

I reply that as much as anyone in the room, I am solidly for entrepreneurism. But if there is one individual in that room whose business plan is shaky, whose commitment is less than one hundred percent, or who in general shouldn't be starting his own business, then by presenting the discouraging facts I believe I am doing him a big favor.

Most new businesses fail, usually within the first few years, yet among any number of first-time entrepreneurs, all believe that they will be among the minority who will make it. A healthy attitude? Certainly, if it can be revised upon further investigation. A realistic assessment of the risk? Not at all.

THREE REASONS WHY THE LEAP IS MADE

Over the years I have observed three reasons people go into business for themselves, two of which are just plain wrong. *The number one reason* people go into business for themselves is that they are unemployed and have a diminishing number of viable alternatives. (Even though this is the worst time to go into business for oneself.)

Particularly in the early 1990s, an increasing share of the baby boom segment of our population—those born between 1946 and 1958—will find themselves becoming entrepreneurs. For some, the decision to own and operate their own businesses will be based on extensive planning, soberly calculated risk, and the opportunity to make a profit. Shockingly, the majority now and throughout the 1990s who venture into their own businesses will do so for the wrong reasons.

The baby boom generation, whose eldest members started turning 40 in the late 1980s, have had to compete with fervor at every stage of their lives, be it for summer jobs, college acceptance, professional employment, mates, housing, etc.

Already documented by such books as *The Plateauing Trap* (Judith Bardwick, Ph.D., AMACOM, 1986) and a host of articles, millions of the seventy-four million members of the baby boom generation, as well as older workers, will be squeezed out of the corporate world and be thrust into an entrepreneurial mode, ready or not. A recent survey of over three hundred human resource directors from the nation's 1,500 largest industrial corporations revealed that twelve million corporate positions are or will soon be considered obsolete.

Bardwick reports that most employees want retraining, but "only 36 percent of those large corporations" offer it. Instead, the majority of employers "put them in jobs that required no new skill, or just got rid of them," among other options. The entrepreneurial boom, and the corresponding record number of business failures (the entrepreneurial bust), will reach even greater heights in the 1990s.

The hundreds of thousands of business failures that have occurred and those that will be occurring are characterized by much more than statistics on a chart. They are also characterized by the not so silent suffering of anxious entrepreneurs and their families. I see no long-term solution to the corporate displacement phenomenon. Each year it will continue to send large numbers of junior and middle managers out into the streets to fend for themselves.

The second most frequent reason people go into business for themselves is that they are good technicians or how-to people in someone else's business. They became cognizant of the errors and shortcomings of the owner/entrepreneur and feel certain that they could do a better job of running the same type of business.

Being proficient at producing widgets or offering X,Y,Z service hardly qualifies a person to manage all of the facets of that business. There are hairdressers who want to set hair but don't know the first thing about preparing a pro forma cash flow statement; auto mechanics who want to fix cars but don't know the first thing about maintaining an inventory system; trainers who want to lead seminars but have no flair for generating new business and think that marketing is something other people do, and public relations advisers who want to attract wealthy clients but have never considered the costs of freelance artists, office supplies, or the telephone bill.

The third reason is the only reason anyone should consider going into business for himself: Here, the aspiring entrepreneur recognizes an opportunity to generate a profit, to provide a service, or sell a product that is needed, that can be differentiated, and that can demand a fair price. This smaller third group of entrepreneurs views going into business as a multifaceted system within which the technical capability that they've mastered plays but one part in the overall success of the venture.

Are those who, facing unemployment, decide to launch a venture doomed to failure? Not necessarily. Each day there are people, in the first or second category, who go into business and who are ultimately successful. Conversely, those in the third category, who have the best chance of succeeding, have no guarantees.

Despite the luck of a few, unless you know you are in the third category—you see the opportunity to make a profit through a sound business idea—you should not entertain starting your own business.

It is possible to start in the first or second category, and through careful planning, study, and the shared knowledge of others, move from the first or second category into the third, i.e., joining the ranks of those who see the opportunity to make a profit. But don't kid yourself—if you find yourself in the first or second category you must change your perspective to increase the odds of success.

THE TOUGHEST BOSS OF ALL

More than a few entrepreneurs have amazed themselves as soon as they have started in business. They become the toughest bosses for whom they have ever worked. The energy that results from a focused, concentrated effort in one's own business enables one to take on more and accomplish more than was ever done at a nine to five job. However, the toughest boss of all is not easy to please.

The late night and weekend hours that you absolutely dreaded when working for someone else start to become commonplace and, strangely enough, desirable. It is after hours, when your employees don't have questions and the phone is not ringing that you can get in three or four uninterrupted hours of concentrated work.

Soon, however, the entrepreneurial lifestyle begins to conflict with all other aspects of your being—watch the game on Sunday or finish the monthly projections? Get out by seven o'clock to watch your daughter's school play? Or press on for just a few minutes more to make sure that report is just right?

Ron Hazelton (name disguised here, and in all cases throughout the book) found that his Long Island rent-a-bay for automobile self-repair was grabbing larger and larger chunks of his time. As the business first struggled, then started to flourish, his family life declined. He and his wife acknowledged that divorce was a possibility. Ron's eight-year-old son, with whom he had always had a wonderful relationship, began experiencing a series of problems including indigestion, bed-wetting, rashes, and temper tantrums. All of these had been non-existent before Ron went into business for himself.

How many new business seminars explore that aspect of entrepreneurship? How many articles in the *New York Times* or the *Wall Street Journal* talk about the downside of entrepreneurism? The answer is a handful a year at best and, not surprisingly, these articles are often skimmed over by those who need them most.

ONE OF LIFE'S GREAT REWARDS

Despite the statistics, or perhaps because of a misreading of them, the lure of entrepreneurism remains strong. I have witnessed great personal reward and deep psychological satisfaction among some of the entrepreneurs with whom I have worked. A few have achieved long-term prosperity. And not one of the four hundred thousand employees of IBM or eight hundred thousand employees of General Motors can experience the depth of feeling that an entrepreneur experiences when making it on his/her own. But, as you will see, it is a long and rocky road!

CHAPTER 2
A Closer Look at Business Failures

There are times in everyone's life when something constructive is born out of adversity. There are times when things seem so bad that you have got to grab your fate by the shoulders and shake it.

—LEE IACOCCA

The primary reason that businesses fail is poor management. The typical entrepreneur who goes into business today is simply underqualified to manage the venture competently. What are some of the crucial factors in a business start-up and where do most entrepreneurs fall short?

Get Up and Go

The entrepreneur must be a self-starting, raring-to-go-on-Monday-morning type person. It doesn't hurt to have boundless energy, but, short of that, one must have at least an energy level far above average. Entrepreneurs must have so strong a desire to run their own businesses that they are willing to work long, hard hours, perhaps for years, in advance of any payoff. Saying that you are willing to work long, hard hours month after month for years on end is one thing. Doing it is quite another. Would-be entrepreneurs consistently grossly underestimate the massive commitment required to make a business successful.

A very large percentage of entrepreneurs experience high levels of stress. Surveys conducted by Laventhol and Horwath, the national accounting firm, indicate that 53 percent of entrepreneurs polled agreed that "ownership of a business leaves little time for friends and family." This finding flies in the face of one of the primary reasons entrepreneurs offer as to why they go into business for themselves—to be in charge of their own time and answer to no one else. Yet nothing could be further from reality. If you want to have *less* time for your family and loved ones, less time for outside interests and hobbies, and less time to relax, then start your own business.

Decision-Making Ability

In operating your own venture, an endless number of decisions must be made: where to locate, what equipment to buy, what marketing tools to employ, who to hire, what to name the firm, where to be listed in the Yellow Pages, etc. The decisions are virtually endless. A booklet distributed by the Small Business Administration, for instance, entitled *Checklist for Going Into Business for Yourself*, lists hundreds of items you'll need to consider.

Since poor management is the fundamental cause of business failure, one might naturally assume that entrepreneurs are eager to enroll in management courses or at least to read a couple of books on the topic, right? Not necessarily so. Most entrepreneurs with whom I have worked are so frazzled and so pressed for time that there is really little possibility that a course or book can make its way into his/her schedule. And even when one can attend a course or read a book, the other distractions and disruptions that abound render the exercise close to futile.

The Personal Touch

The entrepreneurial manager must wear many hats—motivator, salesperson, negotiator, bill payer, loan applicant, to name a few. Entrepreneurs as a species are wont to play their cards particularly close to the chest. Many are lacking in the ability to delegate effectively. Derek du

Toit, an entrepreneur quoted in the *Harvard Business Review*, remarked that "the entrepreneur who starts his own business generally does so because he is a difficult employee . . . his idiosyncrasies do not hurt anybody so long as the business is small, but once the business gets larger, requiring the support and active cooperation of more people, he is at risk if he does not change his approach."

Maybe the above description does not apply to you. However, can you readily respond to advice from others and change direction when necessary? If not, *you* will be your own biggest problem.

Technical Knowledge vs. General Business Knowledge

In Chapter 2, we discussed a fundamental error of those who are functionally or technically competent in a chosen field. Since those who are merely functionally or technically competent have only a portion of the skills necessary to be successful, what else is required? (Note: In Chapter 3, we'll examine if you are "entrepreneurial" material.) It is important to have worked in a business similar to the one you wish to start, and at least have been a foreman or a manager or in some other position of major responsibility.

On the technical side, however, you ought to know the product (or service) and the market from A to Z. The strengths and weaknesses of competitors must be identified and understood. You must have a basic knowledge of accounting, including the key items on the balance sheet and income statement; have a firm grasp of the principles of marketing; and depending on the type of business, be able to supervise all aspects of production.

The vast majority of business failures are due to inadequacy of management. Thus, it is basically you, you, and only you to point at should you not "make it." Yes, one can have bad luck or be penalized by some new government regulation. However, bad luck or government regulations periodically plague all entrepreneurs. It is the entrepreneur's ability to anticipate bad breaks, and have contingency plans for them, that spells the difference between success and failure.

THE BEST OF THE REST

What are the other factors besides incompetent management that contribute to business failure? Attempts to identify causes of business failures are prone to imprecision due to entrepreneurs' frequent inability to assess accurately what it is that "did them in." For example, rather than responding to a survey on the reasons for failure with a statement such as "I was incompetent as a manager," respondents are more likely to reply that the reasons for failure were due to high interest rates, a decline in the economy, too much competition, or some combination thereof. The inability to anticipate these factors, another symptom of managerial incompetence, is rarely cited.

Having made the above distinction, here is a list compiled by Dun & Bradstreet on the causes of business failures in 1985 as reported by entrepreneurs themselves. The percentages sum to over one hundred percent due to multiple responses by many of those surveyed.

"Causes" of Failure, as Reported by Entrepreneurs	
"Economic" Factors	66.4%
Experience	23.1%
Sales	14.2%
Expenses	8.4%
Neglect	2.7%
Customers	1.7%
Capital	1.0%
Assets	0.8%
Disasters	0.6%
Fraud	0.5%

"Economic" factors (meaning the strength and effect of the economy on their businesses) are by far most frequently cited by entrepreneurs. This appears to be the way that entrepreneurs collectively shift the blame for business failures onto the economy. Some of the items cited within "economic" factors include bad profits, loss of market, no consumer spending, and high interest rates. Yet, bad profits or loss of markets can't really be blamed on the economy—even the local economy.

Lack of experience is cited in 23.1 percent of business failures. Subcategories include incompetence, unbalanced experience, lack of line experience, and lack of managerial experience. The third leading "cause" of business failures, sales, at 14.2 percent, had the following as subcategories: inadequate sales, competitively weak, and economic decline, among other lesser items.

Expenses, 8.4 percent, the fourth most prevalent item cited, had the following as subcategories: heavy operating expenses and burdensome institutional debt.

FAILURE INDEX BY INDUSTRY

D&B's failure index (of firms in their data base) is significantly higher in some industries than in others. Here is a look at Dun & Bradstreet's preliminary 1985 failure index by industry:

D&B Business Failure Index By Industry

	Failure Index
Agriculture, Forestry, & Fishing	197
Mining	193
Construction	114
General contractors & operative builders	115
Special trade contractors	103
Total Construction	108
Manufacturing	
Food & kindred products	125
Textile mill products	130
Apparel & other textile products	127
Lumber & wood products	134
Furniture & fixtures	162
Paper & allied products	100
Printing & publishing	94
Chemicals & allied products	126
Petroleum refining	145
Rubber & misc. plastic products	118
Leather & leather products	136
Stone, clay, & glass products	98
Primary metal industries	168
Fabricated metal products	124
Machinery, except electrical	110
Electrical & electronic equipment	154
Transportation equipment	161
Instruments & related products	83
Misc. manufacturing industries	103
Total Manufacturing	119
Transportation & Public Utilities	
Trucking and warehousing	182
Transportation services	119
Communication	123
Electric, gas, & sanitary services	48
Total Transportation & Public Utilities	150

Durable Goods—Wholesale Trade

Motor vehicles & automotive equipment	88
Furniture & home furnishings	127
Lumber & construction materials	102
Sporting goods, toys, & hobby goods	104
Metals & minerals, except petroleum	120
Electrical goods	103
Hardware, plumbing & heating equipment	100
Machinery, equipment, & supplies	113
Miscelleanous durable goods	95
Total Durable Goods	106
Nondurable Goods	94

Retail Trade

Building materials & garden supplies	99
General merchandise stores	70
Food stores	96
Automotive dealers & service stations	80
Apparel & accessory stores	161
Furniture & home furnishing stores	112
Eating & drinking places	145

Miscellaneous Retail Trade

Drug & proprietary stores	38
Liquor stores	70
Used merchandise stores	61
Sporting goods	102
Bookstores	72
Stationery stores	104
Jewelry stores	87
Hobby, toy, & game shops	100
Camera & photographic supply stores	171
Gift, novelty, & souvenir shops	82
Luggage & leather goods stores	102
Sewing, needlework, & piece goods	60
Nonstore retailers	97
Fuel & ice dealers	38
Other retail stores	127
Total Retail Trade	108

Finance, Insurance, & Real Estate

Banking	71
Credit agencies, except banks	56
Security, commodity brokers, & services	137
Insurance carriers	50
Insurance agents, brokers, & services	23
Real estate	73
Combined real estate, insurance, etc.	27
Holding & other investment offices	114
Total Finance, Insurance, & Real Estate	62

Service

Hotels & other lodging places	63

Personal Services

Laundry, cleaning, & garment services	57
Photographic portrait studios	75
Beauty shops	76
Barber shops	85
Shoe repair & hat cleaning shops	45
Funeral services & crematories	19
Miscellaneous personal services	251
Total Personal Services	79

Business Services

Advertising	109
Consumer credit reporting & collection	72
Mail, reproduction & steno services	93
Services to buildings	171
News syndicates	205
Personnel supply services	92
Computer & data processing services	143
Miscellaneous business services	280
Total Business Services..	218

Miscellaneous Services

Automotive repair, services, & garages	103
Miscellaneous repair services	66
Motion pictures, amusement, & recreation	98
Health services	19
Legal services	15
Educational services	18
Social services	73
Museum, botanical & zoological gardens	43
Membership organizations	10
Engineering & architectural services	79
Noncommercial research organizations	5
Accounting, auditing, & bookkeeping services	30
Other services	—
Total Miscellaneous Services	94
Total Services	115

Based on D&B's analysis of their own data base, over 50 percent of service businesses that fail, using the failure index, do so within the first three years in business, compared to retail trade (43.3%); financing, insurance, and real estate (40.7%); and the average of all businesses of 39.7 percent.

One popular notion, based on erroneous information, is that if a business survives a certain number of years, its chances of surviving long term are improved. Not so. In the D&B data base, of reported businesses that failed in 1985, 23.5 percent failed within the sixth to tenth year, and 20.2 percent failed following the tenth year in business.

For those who dream of creating a family-owned business that can be passed on to future generations, Laventhol and Horwath report that only 30 percent of new family businesses last to the second generation and only 15 percent make it to the third. The published rate of successful family business transfers may be far higher than the actual rate. Many of those in the second or third generation inherit businesses of the "living death" variety.

FAILURES BY GEOGRAPHY

Does where you own and operate your business, or where you incorporate your business influence, in any way, the chances for success? Probably so, but to substantiate such findings would require a study beyond the scope of this book. The chart below reveals some statistics about the business failure index throughout regions of the United States.

D&B Business Failure Index by State

	Failure index (preliminary data, 1985)
New England	43.2
Maine	33.2
New Hampshire	26.8
Vermont	29.5
Massachusetts	54.5
Connecticut	39.8
Rhode Island	26.2
Middle Atlantic	55.6
New York	46.6
New Jersey	58.0
Pennsylvania	69.1
East North Central	119.0
Ohio	120.3
Indiana	123.6
Illinois	134.6
Michigan	82.3
Wisconsin	136.4
West North Central	114.4
Minnesota	48.2

Iowa	125.1
Missouri	111.7
North Dakota	55.1
South Dakota	78.8
Nebraska	112.8
Kansas	243.6
South Atlantic	88.2
Maryland	55.7
Delaware	38.6
District of Columbia	34.3
Virginia	106.1
West Virginia	129.1
North Carolina	64.6
South Carolina	45.5
Georgia	87.2
Florida	112.7
East South Central	127.6
Kentucky	139.9
Tennessee	148.2
Alabama	97.2
Mississippi	112.2
West South Central	141.7
Arkansas	128.7
Oklahoma	131.8
Louisiana	163.6
Texas	140.3
Mountain	175.7
Montana	75.8
Idaho	88.6
Wyoming	196.1
Colorado	326.3
New Mexico	128.1
Arizona	89.2
Utah	176.1
Nevada	180.5
Pacific	173.9
Alaska	124.6
Hawaii	115.6
Washington	160.1
Oregon	172.7
California	179.9
Total U.S.	114.0

New England, with a failure index of 43.2, based on preliminary 1985 data, and the Middle Atlantic and South Atlantic states generally have far lower failure indices than the rest of the nation. On the other end of the scale, the Mountain states at 175.7 and the Pacific Coast states at 173.9 lead the nation in this ominous category.

These statistics can be explained in part by examining the demographics of the various regions. Many Pacific Coast states have experienced a rush of entrepreneurial activity and a migration of zestful entrepreneurial types. The Mountain states, including Montana stretching down to Arizona and New Mexico, have experienced dramatic growth in recent years. Colorado, for example, which has experienced a failure index nearly three times that of the rest of the nation, has been particularly attractive to entrepreneurs, especially youthful entrepreneurs who are willing to "risk it all."

Conversely, Atlantic Coast states, particularly the New England states and Middle Atlantic states, with a somewhat more conservative business outlook both on the part of entrepreneurs and the financial institutions that would invest in them, have a lower failure index.

The regional failure index doesn't necessarily reflect the health of the regional or state economies. The prevailing environment may not support an adequate level of risk taking, a factor that ultimately serves to spur the economy.

The failure index of cities follows the path seen at the state and regional level. Houston, a boom town for ten years, followed distantly by Los Angeles, leads the field in failures per ten thousand listed concerns in the D&B data base. The next four positions belong to Chicago, Denver, San Diego, and New York City. On the far end of the scale, Washington, D.C., St. Louis, and Boston each have a low failure index compared to the leaders.

While certain geographic areas have higher business failure indices, on a "micro" basis, geography should have little effect. The fate of any given business is determined much more by the abilities of the entrepreneur than by the region of the country in which it's located.

FAILURE SIZE

Do businesses of a certain size fail more frequently than others? From the mid-1960s to the late 1970s businesses with liabilities between $25,000 and $100,000 had the highest failure index per ten thousand listed concerns. Since 1980, businesses with liabilities between $100,000 and $1,000,000 are failing with more frequency than other businesses.

For nearly thirty years, businesses with liabilities of over

$1,000,000 enjoyed far fewer failures than smaller-sized businesses. In 1984, however, the frequency of failure for larger-sized businesses (based on the D&B index) shot up dramatically, increasing over three hundred percent from the previous year. The apparent trend, and word of caution for entrepreneurs, is that a business's size does not reduce the perils.

The average liability of failed businesses in 1956 was $44,000, rising to $106,000 in 1966, and $313,000 in 1976. As of the end of 1986, the average liability for business failure hovered around the $600,000 mark. The growth in liabilities of failed businesses over the last ten years *exceeds* the rate of inflation. Record numbers of new businesses are being started, record numbers of businesses are failing, and the average dollar losses are increasing dramatically.

FAILURE AMONG THE APPARENTLY SUCCESSFUL

Each year, in its May issue, *Inc.* magazine lists the hundred fastest growing small public companies in America that are less than ten years old, the *Inc.* 100. In 1986, fifty-five of these companies were in manufacturing, twenty-six were in service, six were in mining including oil and gas, six were in wholesale and distribution and seven were in retail. Yet, even the businesses that comprise the elite *Inc.* 100 tend to be money-losing propositions. In fact, thirty out of one hundred showed a net loss for the year, compared to less than 7 percent of Fortune 500 firms for the same period. Professor David Birch of the Massachusetts Institute of Technology, a pioneer in the study of the impact of small business on the nation's economy, observes that "companies that rocket up, often rocket down."

How could so many of the *Inc.* 100, seemingly led by entrepreneurial leaders, experience such results? The answer, unfortunately, is that even successful new ventures are just as affected by bad management and failure to execute. Healthy growth is usually desirable. However, once the initial growth spurt tapers off, these businesses often face excess labor costs, excess capacity, and higher per-unit fixed costs. As *Inc.* writer Tom Richman pointed out in an accompanying *Inc.* article, "the *Inc.* 100 landscape is dotted, if not littered, with the corpses of one-time high flyers . . ."

CHAPTER 3

Are You Entrepreneurial Material?

What you are speaks so loudly I cannot hear what you say.

—RALPH WALDO EMERSON

Many studies have been undertaken in recent years to identify the common denominators of successful entrepreneurs. In looking before you leap into your own business, it is useful to examine those studies and see if your personality and traits are similar to those of successful entrepreneurs.

WHAT IS AN ENTREPRENEUR?

The term entrepreneur has been defined in many ways, including "one who undertakes an enterprise," and "an employer of others." The term is derived from the French word entreprendre, which means "to undertake." My definition of entrepreneur is "an individual who conceives of or offers a product or service that fills a need in the marketplace."

Professor John G. Burch, author of *Entrepreneurship* (John Wiley and Sons, 1986), remarks that "the entrepreneur is the one that undertakes a venture, organizes it, raises capital to finance it, and assumes all or a major portion of the risk." Burch observes that entrepreneurs "appear to be the prime change agents in a society."

Whether this is true or not, entrepreneurs certainly make things happen. They create a business entity that previously did not exist, they produce goods or offer services, they purchase supplies, and they hire people. Some say that entrepreneurs are malcontents or misfits who have a special need to control their own environment. The entrepreneur has been characterized as a loner, maverick, or risk-taker.

Much attention has been focused in recent years on whether entrepreneurs are born or made. University groups, think tanks, and private concerns have shown strong interest in this question. To the extent that entrepreneurial skills can be acquired, and there is strong evidence they can be, a bonanza awaits those who develop effective training programs, seminars, books, and other supporting services. Research indicates that heredity, educational background, work values, family influences, and environmental and cultural conditions influence an individual's decision to become an entrepreneur.

There are over four hundred schools, universities, and adult education programs nationwide offering training or courses on entrepreneurship. Thousands of other institutions, such as the Small Business Administration and professional service firms, as well as research psychologists and consultants can aid you in your quest to become an entrepreneur or simply to know if you have what it takes to be an entrepreneur.

A BAKER'S DOZEN

In working since 1975 with over 225 entrepreneurs in eighteen different states representing sixty different lines of business, I have come to know and appreciate the characteristic traits and values of "entrepreneurial types." In many ways they match the characteristics of pioneers opening up new territories. Here is a list of thirteen traits generally found among individuals who have started their own ventures and become successful at it.

1. **Motivated to achieve**—Entrepreneurs are basically goal-oriented and have the ability to enroll others around them in pursuit of their goals. Entrepreneurs are less likely to be concerned with maintaining a high level of social interaction. They are strongly influenced by the desire to achieve the goals and objectives that they have established.

2. **Reward seekers**—Entrepreneurs have a need to be visibly rewarded for their creativity and risk taking. The reward or payoff could take the form of profits, community status, admiration of others, and confirmation of being "right."

3. **Calculated risk-takers**—Entrepreneurs thrive on a certain degree of risk. They accept the challenge of exposing themselves to risk situations, and then set about to reduce risks by planning and successful execution. Also, they have a built-in sense of what represents inordinate risk.

4. **Ability to organize**—Even amidst desks cluttered with papers, entrepreneurs have the capability to create systems that accomplish the task at hand. They recognize that achieving challenging goals is directly related to their ability to both plan and organize.

5. **Maintain a healthy outlook**—Entrepreneurs are basically positive people with an optimistic view of life. They are open to new possibilities and have a way of recovering quickly from setbacks. They achieve some sense of satisfaction when goals are reached, but then quickly set new goals.

6. **Commitment**—Successful entrepreneurs maintain a "whatever it takes" attitude in making their ventures successful. They derive a sense of satisfaction from their work that makes the long hours palatable. While some could be classified as workaholics, most entrepreneurs could be aptly classified as "achievement-aholics."

7. **High energy**—Entrepreneurs seem to have high energy. They get sick far less often than is normal, perhaps because they simply can't afford to become sick. They are the most energetic, vibrant people in the companies they have started, however large their size. They are among the most energetic in the organizations they left before starting their own ventures. They have a sense of well being that enables them to "drop back" before jeopardizing their health.

8. **Roll with the punches**—They are tough cookies when the situation calls for it, but are able to modify their behavior to meet changing conditions. Entrepreneurs have a resiliency and durability that enables

29

them to bend and not break. They are willing to stray from the plan when it is evident that there is a better way.

9. **Maintain vocal authority**—Successful entrepreneurs sound as if they are definitely in charge. They generally have good communication and listening skills. They are comfortable when interacting with and directing others. While their appearance may not always suggest "leader," their vocal authority does.

10. **Believability**—Winning entrepreneurs have an aura of genuineness, especially in the nonverbal cues others receive from them. They are able to open doors more quickly because their believability stimulates cooperation by others.

11. **Accept Responsibility**—Successful entrepreneurs recognize that their destiny is largely controlled by themselves. They readily accept responsibility for the success of their ventures and generally do not assign blame to outside factors. Roadblocks are handled as challenges, as opposed to being used as reasons why something could not be done.

12. **Accurate self-assessment**—Entrepreneurs know what they do well and have identified those areas in which they are weak. They use this knowledge to assemble the resources that complement their own capabilities. Some are able to view their weaknesses as additional challenges that must be overcome (more on weakness below).

13. **Perseverance**—Last and certainly not least, they are willing to continue when all else says "stop." Rejection may temporarily slow them down, but isn't sufficient to put them out of the race. Successful entrepreneurs are willing to pick themselves up again and again and press on.

COMMON WEAKNESSES?

Each of the strengths that I list above can be taken to extremes and become an ingredient for failure. For example, the entrepreneur committed to working hard may abandon family and friends who served as an essential support system and balancing mechanism. Without such systems in place, the entrepreneur may find himself working to achieve goals that have no real meaning in the overall context of his life. The excessively organized entrepreneur may waste valuable time and resources fine-tuning procedures when that time could be better spent, for example, generating new business.

Here are some negative traits that I've even observed among

successful entrepreneurs. They serve as points of comparison with your own behavior.

1. **Set up unrealistic time frames.** While entrepreneurs are generally perseverant, they also tend to be in a hurry. They want to achieve challenging goals quickly and often underestimate the time and resources that will be necessary (see Chapters 4, 8, 14).

2. **Keep cards too close to the chest.** Many entrepreneurs do not delegate authority, tasks, or responsibilities sufficiently to subordinates. Also many maintain hidden-agenda items that they attempt to accomplish by themselves.

3. **Tolerate too many interruptions.** In the desire to handle everything, many entrepreneurs leave themselves wide open to interruption. The primary culprits in this department are the telephone and the unscheduled appointment.

4. **Work without a plan.** Many entrepreneurs prepare an extensive business plan at the start of a business. Subsequently, this plan is rarely if ever updated or revamped. Entrepreneurs have a tendency toward "seat of the pants" management.

5. **Not doing homework.** In their eagerness to get a business off and running, or to develop a new marketing campaign for a product or service, many entrepreneurs tend to proceed headlong into untested waters without sufficiently researching the prevailing environment.

ENTREPRENEURISM AND YOU—AN INTROSPECTIVE ANALYSIS

We have discussed many common denominators among successful entrepreneurs as well as some widely observed negative traits. You may ask, "Is there a way to assess my potential as an entrepreneur?" To do so we will look at three basic areas including:

1. personal resource identification
2. personal behavioral characteristics
3. personal strengths and weaknesses

1. **Personal resource identification**—What is your formal education and how applicable is it to your intended venture? This need not be a one-to-one match; however, some correlation is certainly desirable.

Next, what is your specific experience and what lessons have you learned, and how will they apply in the proposed venture? A similar evaluation should be made of your specific skills or talents. What other specific knowledge do you have that will support your venture and, specifically, how does it apply? Finally, a biggie—who will fill in if you become seriously ill?

This risk of starting a new venture is increased to the degree that your personal skills and resources fail to support the proposed venture. For example, if your background is in computer-aided design and you want to start a company that distributes cassette tapes, you are effectively starting a new business in a new field for you. I regard this risk as a double whammy—you are starting a new business (one whammy) in a new field (another whammy) for you. If your background is in cassette tape distribution, then the risk of starting a business in this field is a single whammy—you are starting a new business (one whammy) in a field in which you have significant experience (no whammies).

Single-whammy risks are generally acceptable, given no other extenuating circumstances. Double-whammy risks are never acceptable and are subject to astronomical failure rates. When you already have experience running your own business and want to add a new product, a new service, or start a new business, the risk is acceptable. This is not nearly as risky as the double-whammy risk that occurs when someone who has never operated a business chooses to do so in a field new to him.

2. **Personal behavioral characteristics**—Are you generally perseverant, patient? Do you describe yourself, or do others, as a creative type? Now the telling question, do you believe deep down to the marrow in your bones that you will be successful? If the answer isn't an unqualified "yes," either entrepreneurism isn't for you, or you don't have a viable venture in mind.

3. **Personal strengths and weaknesses**—Are you: persuasive, credible, flexible, efficient?

Do you have the ability to maintain effective working relationships with other people? Are you able to establish priorities? Have you gauged your own weaknesses and are you prepared to get help when necessary? Also, are you able to "make do" in a pinch? If not, this is cause for concern.

32

BOUNCING YOUR IDEAS OFF OTHERS

Before formally constructing a business plan, it makes good sense to bounce your ideas off others. Identify five to eight people whom you respect and trust and ask them if they think you have what it takes to become an entrepreneur. Don't assume that you already know what the answers will be.

If you really feel like getting some good feedback, ask them what they think your ten greatest strengths would be in operating your own venture. Next, ask them for a candid review of what your ten greatest weaknesses would be. If the people you have asked are reluctant to candidly assess your weaknesses, or offer you positive type weaknesses, press them on this issue; you need to have this information.

Going a step further, identify other personal contacts in the community, some of which can be included in the first list of people you contacted, who can help you determine if your proposed venture is sound. People to contact include teachers, instructors or professors, accountants, experienced entrepreneurs, executives, SBA assistance officers and SCORE (Service Corps of Retired Executives) and anyone else whose experience leads you to believe that s/he would serve as a useful sounding board.

The business world is fraught with the wretched failures of hundreds of thousands of entrepreneurs who "just knew" that their business ideas were "can't miss" ventures. You will need as much qualified input and advice *before* you start a business as you will need while actually operating it.

WHAT IF YOUR IDEA HAS MERIT?

If most of the people with whom you speak agree that your idea has merit, your next step will be to produce a comprehensive business plan (next chapter). You cannot divorce your quest and predisposition to be an entrepreneur from the soundness of your proposed venture. The two go hand in hand, are inextricably intertwined, and will unavoidably be perceived as a package to everyone you encounter.

What are some of the management challenges you will face (Chapter 5)? What kind of financing (Chapter 6) will be necessary to launch this venture? Most new business are slightly to chronically underfinanced. The business plan, financial statements, and cash flow projections, along with your managerial capability, literally become your keys to influencing others to take an active financial interest in your venture.

Whether or not you are entrepreneurial material depends on your ability to produce a sound plan, counterbalance your weaknesses, line up necessary financing, and get qualified help. But clearing all those hurdles is just the tip of the iceberg.

CHAPTER 4

The Business Plan Monster

It is not enough to do your best; sometimes it is necessary to do what is required.

—WINSTON CHURCHILL

In the prebusiness phase the vast majority of your efforts should be directed towards the preparation of a comprehensive business plan. This is no easy undertaking and can easily take from 250 to 500 hours to complete in detail. Not many entrepreneurs like to hear that they will be spending six, nine, or twelve solid weeks on preparing a business plan, yet to do the job properly that is what will be required. Still, it is extraordinary that hundreds of thousands of ventures are launched each year with no plans, or inadequate ones.

Specifically, those seeking outside financing must, and everyone else should, prepare business plans that include multiyear projections, a detailed marketing plan, and a description of the management's expertise, among many other items. Particularly when preparing a business plan to secure external financing, you must determine an amount needed for seed capital—money that will be required to open the business, secure equipment and inventory, and provide at least three months of working capital.

SHELDON'S LAWS

Richard Sheldon, a Harvard M.B.A. and the owner of more than a dozen businesses based in the mid-Connecticut area, created two simple laws, Sheldon's Laws. These laws universally apply to entrepreneurs and are of particular importance in preparing the business plan.

> Sheldon's Three-Times Law: When starting a new business, things take three times as long as you think they will.
>
> Sheldon's Two-Times Law: When starting a new business, you will need twice as much money as you think you will.

These three-times and two-times laws have proven amazingly accurate over the years. Let's look at each in detail.

The three-times law means that the revenue projected for Year One will probably not be achieved until Year Three. The number of new customers or contracts you think you will win in the first year will probably take you three years. If you need to hire staff and are eager to assemble a confident crew within two months, you'll probably take six months, and so on.

I have spoken about the three-times rule and have seen would-be entrepreneurs mildly shake their heads saying, "No, I can do it in less." Nobody takes the three-times law at face value. People find it axiomatic and illustrative, but they don't see it as having any application in their business planning.

The two-times law, for most people, is even harder to fathom. While it might be difficult to predict how long it will take to reach certain goals, surely one can tabulate the funds required to accomplish a task! Guess again.

As consumers, we get accustomed to having things always cost a little more than anticipated. As entrepreneurs, with the responsibility for expenditures on items with which we are not familiar, or have not previously purchased, innumerable surprises await. Expense items that you are apt to overlook, that easily find their way into your wallet, include (but are not limited to) the following:

- Excess maintenance and repair of key equipment—These always have a way of escalating. See Chapter 8, Cost and Operation Control.

- Help wanted advertisements in the classifieds—one four-inch-by-two-column advertisement in the Sunday classified section of your city newspaper costs several hundred dollars. If you have to run the ad more than once, and usually you will, this rapidly climbs into the four-figure range.

- Adding a second telephone line—With as few as three calls per hour or three employees, you will probably need to add a second telephone line. Your business telephone expense can be five to ten times or more than your personal telephone expense.

- Snow removal—When you worked for X,Y,Z Corp. and drove in on winter days, the parking lot or garage was ready to accommodate you. In operating your own venture, removing the snow from the parking lot becomes another minor expense of being in business. The problem is, minor expenses will be in abundance.

- Office cleaning—You are certainly not going to take the time to clean your office, and you really can't ask your employees to do it. Cost of cleaning your office is based on your square footage and the frequency of the cleaning.

- Excessive photocopying—Unless you maintain very strict control and have outrageous self-discipline, the cost of copier paper and supplies will eat into your checkbook. Even in a two-person outfit, your copying costs are likely to be above $1,000 per year, if not much higher.

- Bad debts and collection expense—A real crusher if you have never experienced this before. See Chapter 11, Passing the Collection Plate, to gain a real sense of how insidious the collection problem can be for small businesses.

- Pilferage of small office supplies—Your employees will rob you blind, because many will regard pilferage of small office supplies a job perquisite. See Chapter 7, Personnel Problems and Chapter 8, Cost and Operation Control.

The capital that will be required to sustain effective marketing campaigns, install a proper accounting system, and be computerized, is *always* greater than first estimated, and in many cases more than double.

If you doubt the validity of the two-times law, recall that nearly 30 percent of the firms listed in the *Inc.* 100 were in the red. (Note: the *Inc.* listing is based upon percentage increase in growth rate, and not on profitability.) Earlier in the life of the businesses listed in *Inc.* 100, the *majority* also had a negative net income. Often the fastest growing firms don't show a profit for several years.

Below is an adapted outline of *the* traditional business plan, recommended in several leading texts, covering all of the components typically required as a prelude to financing a business. Please keep Sheldon's Laws in mind as you consider the components of the business plan.

BUSINESS PLAN OUTLINE

I. Introduction and Statement of the Business Concept
    A. General statement of purpose and objectives
    B. Historical background
        1. Date of organization
        2. Present legal structure (date and state of incorporation, if incorporated)
        3. Major changes in business purpose, objectives, or strategies
    C. Brief description of the market(s)
    D. Brief description of the product(s)/service(s)
II. External Environment and Industry Analysis
    A. Size and nature of the market
        1. Detailed definition of overall market(s)
        2. Market segment(s)
        3. Rationale for the market segment(s) selected
        4. Factors influencing demand
            a. Customers, customer need(s), profiles
            b. Frequency of purchase
            c. Size of individual transaction
            d. Influence of advertising, packaging, and display

      e. Price and customer sensitivity to price changes
      f. Income of target population
      g. Relationship to complementary products
      h. Seasonal and cyclical influences

  B. Relationships with other institutions (governments, unions)
  C. Laws pertaining to the enterprise
  D. Competition
    1. Nature of close competition
    2. Indirect competition
    3. Nature of competitive practices within the industry (price, quality, advertising, technology, service, and other competitive forces)
      a. Number and size of firms
      b. Vertical and horizontal integration within firms
      c. Location of firms (foreign, domestic, local)
    4. Nature of cooperative practices within the industry

III. Product(s)/Service(s) Offered and to Be Offered
  A. Detailed description of the product(s)/service(s)
  B. Assessment of competitive advantages and disadvantages
    1. Technological position (obsolescence, patent, copyright protection)
    2. Design, styling, trademark
    3. Quality, quality control, product life, durability
    4. Completeness of product/service line
    5. Location
    6. Relationship with suppliers
    7. Distribution
    8. Costs and pricing
    9. Services

IV. Growth Strategy
  A. Approach to and entry into new markets
  B. Approach to growth and maintenance of market share
  C. Five-year revenue forecasts

V. Marketing
  A. Geographical coverage of the markets
  B. Channels of distribution and methods of sale
  C. Type, quality, and availability of salespersons and distributors
  D. Training and deployment of salespersons and distributors

E. Advertising and public relations
F. Equipment required
G. Organization and personnel other than salesmen and distributors

VI. Operations
A. Location
B. Required facilities
C. Required equipment
D. Raw materials (sources and cost)
E. Work subcontracted (sources and cost)
F. Inventory and inventory control
G. Quality and quality control
H. Organization and personnel
   1. Type, expertise, and availability of personnel
   2. Industrial relations
   3. Compensation

VII. Research and Development
A. Planning and control
B. Organization and personnel
C. Equipment

VIII. Finance
A. Planning and control
B. Organization and personnel
C. Equipment

IX. Management
A. Senior management personnel
   1. Résumés and statement of qualifications
   2. Functions
   3. Level of compensation
   4. Employment contracts, noncompete agreements, buy-out agreements, and patent assignment
B. Equipment

X. Organizational Chart

XI. Financial Analysis
A. Summary of company's financial condition
   1. Prior capital contributions
   2. Major current stockholders and how they acquired their equity
   3. Current debt, lenders, and terms
   4. Use of prior capital

B.   Historical and pro forma (three to five years) income statement and balance sheets

C.   Historical and pro forma (three to five years) cash flow

D.   Required investment

E.   Return on investment

F.   Financial comparison with similar firms

G.   Schedule of disbursements

H.   Performance mileposts

XII. Risk Analysis

A.   Qualitative risk analysis (statement of the major areas of risk and the steps taken to deal with them)

B.   Quantitative risk analysis

1. Break-even points

a. Fixed costs

b. Variable costs

c. Semivariable costs

2. Payback period

3. Probabilistic forecast

C.   Disaster plan

XIII. Plan Update

A.   How, When, and Who

Let's briefly walk through some of the elements in the business plan outline and discuss the formidable amount of research and data you will have to gather to complete it.

IA. Statement of Purpose—This should be formal and no more than one page. This statement must convince financial sources and potential investors that your business is or can be viable.

IB3. Major Changes in Business Purpose—If the plan you are preparing represents an updated plan from the original one and your focus has shifted, the rationale should be described here.

IC. Brief Description of Market—In one concise paragraph, who do you serve and what do you offer? Details should be provided in later sections.

IIA. Size and Nature of the Market—How large is the market? What special needs does this market have? Why have you chosen to serve this market? (See Chapter 13, Marketing Mania.)

IIA4. Factors Influencing Demand—This important section requires a concise description of customers, how they buy, when they buy, and what influences their purchasing decisions. Also, what is the importance of price? Are there other products and services that influence purchases (i.e., the number of automobile tires sold is directly related to the number of automobiles on the road)? Are there seasonal and cyclical fluctuations? In the retail business or when working with government entities, for example, the time of year profoundly affects how much business can be generated.

IIC. Laws Pertaining to the Enterprise—You must indicate your knowledge of the prevailing legal environment vis-a-vis your industry or occupation.

IID. Competition—What are the names, approximate market shares, and competitive advantages of direct competitors, and of indirect competitors? Then discuss what will you do to be competitive.

IIIA. Detailed Description of Products/Services Offered—This section must be accompanied by photos, brochures, "spec" sheets, standard descriptive materials, or other printed descriptions.

IVA. Approach to and Entry Into New Markets—This section requires foresight; new markets may not have been considered in the prebusiness planning stage.

IVC. Five-Year Revenue Forecast—A major stumbling block with entrepreneurs, the revenue forecast that includes an estimation of both gross revenues and expenses must be supported by detailed financial information. However, as previously mentioned, it is extremely difficult, even with help, to determine and estimate the various *expenses* you'll encounter. More on this in Chapters 6 and 8. Forecasting for the first year is bad enough. The second through fifth years, however, require vision, mixed with reality, which is founded on reliable assumptions.

VA. Geographic Coverage of the Markets—Here you must precisely define your trade radius, be it a neighborhood, town, state, section of a country, the whole country, continent, section of the world, or planet earth.

VB. Channels of Distribution—How will your goods and services be received by the customer/client?

VD. Training and Deployment of Salespersons and Distributors— What type of in-house or external program will you use to insure that your company's approach to sales is professional? (Chapter 13)

VIB.,C. Facilities and Equipment Required—You must list each item that will be required in your business including its cost (purchase or lease) and expected life. Also you must describe in detail the office, plant, showroom, or warehouse in which you will be located and its specific features that support your operation.

VIE. Work Subcontracted—Who will you be using and what will they charge? What is the reputation of subcontractors, and how long have they been in business?

VIF. Inventory and Inventory Control—Of more than ten types of inventory systems, you must describe in detail which one you will employ and how this will insure minimum losses due to theft, damaged goods, and excess holding costs.

VIG. Quality and Quality Control—Manufacturers must provide a detailed description of various inspection, spot checking, and tagging procedures you will install to assure high-quality products. Service firms must also describe their quality control measures.

VIH. Organization and Personnel—This section requires a list of every person who will be working for you, the background and expertise of each person, and the wages you intend to pay them.

VII. Research and Development—If applicable, this section requires the same level of detail as that provided for your marketing and financial systems.

IXA. Senior Management Personnel—This section is examined very closely by those reading your business plan. Lack of competent management is the single greatest cause of small-business failures.

X. Organizational Chart—Even if you are a one-person company, graphically depict your relationship to suppliers, creditors, legal counsel, part-time staff, secretarial services, etc.

XIA. Summary of Company's Financial Condition—When seeking debt financing for start-up, you must discuss your ability to raise equity capital. When raising equity capital, all the other items in section 11 assume even greater importance.

XIB. Historical and Pro Forma Financial Statements—This requires an item-by-item listing of all income statement and balance sheet components. If you are unfamiliar with financial analysis you will definitely need help with this.

XIE. Return on Investment—There are several ROI formulas routinely sought by financial officers and investors. This section will be read very closely; there is little margin for error.

XIF. Financial Comparison—This section requires a comparison of your balance sheet and income statements with industry norms.

XIG. Schedule of Disbursements—If your business plan is being developed for the express purpose of generating funds, you must prepare a schedule precisely indicating when and where each dollar will be spent.

XII. Risk Analysis—What can go wrong? What is likely to go wrong? This section should be based on the general experience of firms in your industry and the specifics related to your venture. Many entrepreneurs are reluctant to mention that anything can go wrong—an ostrichlike approach to starting and operating a venture.

XIIB. Quantitative Risk Analysis—Such computations as break even points and payback periods are a standard part of business plans and help indicate your awareness of what is required in order to achieve profitability.

Related to no. 12 above, what type of insurance coverage and contingency plans will be set in place in order to handle the unforeseen, such as accidents on the job, fire, theft, your illness, etc.? Depending on your state, many forms of insurance are now mandatory and should be described in your plan. The following forms should be included:

- Key executive
- Disability
- Group health
- Group life
- Workman's compensation
- Fidelity bond
- Business interruption
- Crime insurance
- Fire
- Liability
- Automobile

If you're a manufacturer, you'll need product liability insurance. If you're a professional service provider or in the medical profession you'll need malpractice insurance.

THAT'S NOT ALL, FOLKS

There are other supporting documents that enhance a business plan and make it a more complete package. You will have prepare or gather the following:

- Job descriptions—of key management and technical positions
- Personal financial statements—self, and key stockholders
- Credit reports—from suppliers, lending institutions and credit bureaus
- Letters of reference—from former employers and those with whom you've worked
- Letters of intent—those that are interested in buying your products or services
- Copies of leases—for space and equipment
- Legal documents—such as incorporation paper, franchise agreements, permits, etc.

Fortunately, many components of the business plan don't change, or change infrequently, thereby reducing some of your maintenance responsibilities. However, those that do change and need continuous and particular attention include:

II.   External Environment and Industry Analysis
V.   Marketing
XI.   Financial Analysis and
XII. Risk Analysis

Note: Common pitfalls faced by entrepreneurs in preparing a marketing plan—the largest and most important subset of a business plan—are discussed in Chapter 13, Marketing Mania.

THE SBA BUSINESS PLAN

Every year thousands of first-time entrepreneurs turn to the SBA for assistance. Imagine that you've spent hundreds of hours to complete a solid long-term plan. You've been turned down by several banks, and now, like thousands of others, you approach the SBA for financial assistance. Some of the information sought by the SBA is different from what you gathered for your own business plan. You'll now have to spend at least another forty hours or more completing their form. Here is a *streamlined* look at the SBA's business plan:

U.S. Small Business Administration
Business Plan and Qualifications Résumé
(Each item should be completed; if none or not applicable so state.)

1. Firm identification:

Name _____

Trade name _____

Address_____
Street   P.O. Box

_____
City   County   State Zip

Business phone_____ _____ Home phone_____ _____
     Area Code Number   Area Code Number

Type of business _____ SIC Code _____

Employees' identification number _____ Tax exemption no. _____

Number of employees: _____ as of _____

Indicate if supply, service, construction, or concession _____

Month and year business established _____

Fiscal year ends _____

Is concern organized for profit? Yes ☐ No ☐

Is concern associated in any way with a nonprofit organization?
               Yes ☐ No ☐
If yes, specify name of nonprofit organization and the nature of the association _____
_____
_____

Do concern and affiliates meet small business size standard as defined in Part 121 SBA Rules and Regulations? Yes ☐ No ☐ If answer is *no*, Divestiture Agreement must be submitted.

II. List other types and locations of business in which firm is or has recently been engaged.

Type of business _____

Address of facility: _____

_____

Presently operating: Yes ☐ No ☐ If operating, how long? _____

III. List all entities in which owners, directors, officers, partners, and managers of applicant have a financial interest or hold a management or board position. If none, so state.

Name of Entity	Name of Person	Position Held	% of Ownership
_____	_____	_____	_____
_____	_____	_____	_____
_____	_____	_____	_____
_____	_____	_____	_____

IV. Company History: (Narrative of purpose, chronological development, problems, and successes.)

V. Product or service: (Narrative of characteristics, uses, and applicability to commerical market. Nature of work performed with own forces, area of operations.)

VI.　A.　Management:(A copy of this form must be completed by all directors, officers, and senior management personnel.)

1. Name _____ 2. Age _____ 3. Sex _____

4. Marital status _____ 5. Social security number _____

6. Military serial number _____

7. Present position (Include description of duties)

8. Other jobs and positions held and salaries

9. Formal schooling

10. Technical training and qualifications

11.. Management training

12. Military experience

(a)	Branch of Service	Place of Service	Period of Service	MOS	Rank
	_____	_____	_____	_____	_____
	_____	_____	_____	_____	_____

(b)   Service schools attended and date of attendance

_____

_____

_____

B. List professional, management, and technical resource support to be received by your company. (Attach copies of all Management and Technical Support Agreements.)

Name	Address	Phone	Service Performed	Compen-sation to be paid
____	____	____	____	____
____	____	____	____	____
____	____	____	____	____
____	____	____	____	____
____	____	____	____	____

C. Diagram organizational chart of firm.

VII.   Marketing:
A. Market area:

B. Market potential:

C. Commercial customers:

D. Government customers: (Include name and phone number of contracting officers and small business specialist contacted.)

E. Competitors

F. Advantage over competitors

G. Pricing and bidding procedures (Attach sample of pricing and bidding documents.)

H. Sales forecast by product or service category

I. Sales and distribution plan: (including advertising pricing, credit terms, etc.)

J. Business plan graph (break even point)

Sales
Dollars
(000)

$

$

$

$

Production capacity

1st yr.   2nd yr.   3rd yr.   4th yr.

K. Break even chart (reflect income from sales, fixed cost, variable cost and
    break even point.)

Cost in
Dollars

0

100

50

Percentage of plant capacity in operation

51

VIII. Production:
   A. Plant: (Include location, total square footage, and layout and sketch of office and storage areas. Also include copy of lease, deed or proposed lease.)

   B. Equipment:

Quantity	Description	Age	Buying or Leasing	Cost

   C. Equipment layout and production flow plan:

   D. Supervisory personnel (names and responsibilities):

   E. Labor skill and source (detailed list by classification, number, and pay rate):

Skill Classification	Number	Pay Rate	Source

   F. Materials used, source of supply, and average delivery time:

   G. Shipping facilities and accessibility to transportation:

   H. Quality control system:

   I. Workforce classified as disadvantaged and training programs:

52

J.   Expansion capability:

IX.   Operational plan:

X.   Financial

Attach year-end and current business balance sheet on applicant and affiliates, year-end and current profit and loss statements on applicant and affiliates, aging of accounts receivable and payables on applicant, monthly cash flow for twelve months on applicant and annual detail projection for two years on applicant.

A.   Sales history (Applicant)

	FY_____	FY_____	FY_____	Year-end to Date as of _____
Commercial	_____	_____	_____	_____
Government other _____	_____	_____	_____	_____
Total _____	_____	_____	_____	_____

B.   Profits or Losses (Applicant)

FY_____	FY_____	FY_____	Year-end to Date as of _____
_____	_____	_____	_____

C.   Projection (Applicant)

	1st Year	2nd Year	3rd Year	4th Year
Commercial sales	_____	_____	_____	_____
Government other	_____	_____	_____	_____
TOTAL	_____	_____	_____	_____

D. Condensed balance sheets history (applicant)

Current as of _____		FY Ending 19_____	
C/A_____	C/L_____	C/A_____	C/L_____
F/A_____	LT/L_____	F/A_____	LT/L_____
O/A_____	N/W_____	O/A_____	N/W_____
TOTAL_____	_____	_____	_____

FY Ending 19_____		FY Ending 19_____	
C/A_____	C/L_____	C/A_____	C/L_____
F/A_____	LT/L_____	F/A_____	LT/L_____
O/A_____	N/W_____	O/A_____	N/W_____
TOTAL_____	_____	_____	_____

Key: C/A—current assets O/A—other assets LT/L—Long-term liabilities

F/A—Fixed assets C/L—current liabilities N/W—Net worth

E. Sales history (affiliates—sponsors)

Name of Affiliate _____

	FY_____	FY_____	FY_____	Year-end to date as of _____
Commercial_____	_____	_____	_____	
Government_____	_____	_____	_____	
TOTAL	_____	_____	_____	_____

F. Condensed balance sheets (affiliates—sponsors)

Name of affiliate _____

| Current as | FY Ending |
| of _____ | 19_____ |

C/A_____ C/L_____   C/A_____ C/L_____

F/A_____ LT/L_____   F/A_____ LT/L_____

O/A_____ N/W_____   O/A_____ N/W_____

TOTAL_____ _____   _____ _____

| FY Ending | FY Ending |
| 19_____ | 19_____ |

C/A_____ C/L_____   C/A_____ C/L_____

F/A_____ LT/L_____   F/A_____ LT/L_____

O/A_____ N/W_____   O/A_____ N/W_____

TOTAL_____ _____   _____ _____

XI. Other pertinent information:
A. Contracts or jobs in-house

Customer & Representative	Description	Amount ($)	% Completed	Scheduled Completion
_____	_____	_____	_____	_____
_____	_____	_____	_____	_____
_____	_____	_____	_____	_____

B. Average monthly billings—$

C. Record of surety and fidelity bonds:

Date	Job or Person	Type of Bond	Amount	Surety Company	Agent or Agency

D. Contracts or jobs completed within the last two years

Customer	Description	Amount ($)

E. Schedule of insurance:

Company	Coverage	Amount	Expiration Date	Agent or Agency

F. Bank and trade reference:

Name and Address	Contact Person and Position
_____	_____
_____	_____

G. Availability of credit and financial assistance:

Source	Amount	Terms	Degree of Commitment (Attach any documentation of commitment)
_____	_____	_____	_____
_____	_____	_____	_____
_____	_____	_____	_____

H. List of loans or loan guarantees provided by the Small Business Administration

Names and address of lender	Loan Number	Original Amount of loan	Amount Outstanding
_____	_____	_____	_____
_____	_____	_____	_____
_____	_____	_____	_____

I. Outline of business goals: (necessary to become competitive)

Annual sales $_____   Current ratio _____ to _____

Annual profits $_____   Debt to net _____ to _____
                                   worth ratio

Bondability $_____   Estimated number of _____ to _____
                                   years to become competitive

J. Additional equipment necessary to conduct competitive business:

Description	Purchase cost	Lease cost
_____	$_____	$_____
_____	$_____	$_____
_____	$_____	$_____
_____	$_____	$_____
_____	$_____	$_____
TOTAL	$_____	$_____per mo.

K. Other resources needed to become competitive:

Type	Amount	Anticipated source
_____	_____	_____
_____	_____	_____
_____	_____	_____

L. Licenses and certificates in effect:

Type	Amount	Place of issue
_____	_____	_____
_____	_____	_____
_____	_____	_____

M. List trade association and other organizations of which company is a member.

N. Labor agreements in effect.

O. Contracts with suppliers

P. List lawsuits in force or pending

Q. Patents, royalties, etc.

R. Product research and development

S. Annual sales volume in dollars required for company to break even. $____

GATHERING DUST

Three or four months into the business a funny thing happens. That sterling gem of a plan, sitting in the top left-hand drawer of the entrepreneur's desk, barely sees the light of day. Not by design or mischievous intent, the plan ends up buried in a drawer or file, and ages gracefully because the typical entrepreneur does not embrace it as a working document. It was something that had to be done in order to get the business up and running, but in the daily quest to stamp out forest fires, the plan is simply lost among the ashes.

Every once in a while, though, along comes an entrepreneur who not only prepares a gem of a plan, but also examines it periodically. However, most plans quickly diminish in value. The reality of operating the business is usually so dissimilar to the projections, strategies, and activities called for in the plan that it is simply not viable as a working document, unless it is updated regularly.

So the question becomes, does the plan get updated when necessary? Now, here is a most telling point regarding entrepreneurism and long-term planning. It is based on my experience in working on site with hundreds of firms in the last ten years and in lecturing and counseling thousands of others. Three to nine months following the start of a business, less than 5 percent commit the time, effort, and energy to recompose their business plans, based on experiences gained and a clearer understanding of the prevailing environment.

Inadequate business planning and updating is a prevalent, major pitfall among entrepreneurs. I often have asked entrepreneurs why they have been negligent in maintaining an updated business plan. The responses are reflected by the following statements:

"I have been meaning to do it. . ."
"There just never seems to be enough time."

"Every time I start I get interrupted."

"It is such a large task I just keep putting it off."

"I am not sure I see the real value in it."

"I am planning on doing it at the end of the month."

"I know I need to do it, but it's too much work."

"Once I take care of X, Y, Z, I plan on getting to it."

When we read other people's excuses we see how lame they are. Nevertheless, even as you say to yourself, *"I'll* maintain an updated plan," the odds are overwhelming that you won't.

Why is business planning so arduous a task that most entrepreneurs make optional? There are several reasons, including:

1. The sheer number of elements that go into a complete plan is awesome.

2. There may be several elements of planning that cannot be presently addressed.

3. Many of the components are interrelated, consequently a change in one necessitates readdressing other components.

4. The business plan for any business is a unique document—one may not simply borrow from the plans of others.

5. There are many supporting documents to gather.

From all vantage points, preparing and maintaining an updated business plan is no small task. Several texts are available on how to prepare a business plan, including:

*Business Package,*Washington, D.C.: Department of Housing and Urban Development, 1979.

Business Planning Guide by David H. Bangs, Jr. and William R. Osgood, Portsmouth, N.H.; Upstart Publishing Co., Inc., 1979.

How to Write a Winning Business Plan by Joseph R. Mancuso, New York: Center for Entrepreneurial Management, 1985.

New Venture Creation: A Guide to Small Development by Jeffrey A. Timmons, Leonard E. Smollen, and Alexander Dingee, Homewood, IL.: Richard D. Irwin, Inc. 1977.

Entrepreneurship and Small Business Management by Kenneth R. Van Voorhis, Boston: Allyn and Bacon, 1980.

CHAPTER 5

Management Misconceptions

When love and skill work together, expect a miracle.

—JOHN RUSKIN

The myth of being the boss has drawn many an eager beaver having no clear perception of what it means to run a business. The typical would-be entrepreneur has a vision of how it is going to be: complete independence; flexible hours; a staff of well-trained, motivated employees; no more red tape; use of everyone else's capital. Many first timers project a healthy profit figure for the first year of operations. This chapter explores some of the common myths about entrepreneurship.

Being your own boss means that a tremendous amount of time must be spent on a never-ending variety of duties. Even if business is operating well, the demand on the entrepreneur is usually so great that there is little time to learn about or to improve methods that could further develop the business. Such an enormous investment of personal energy, resources, and identity is required to make the business a go that many entrepreneurs become one and the same with their businesses. Their identities become inextricably intertwined with their ventures.

Running a business can be a draining, exhausting experience that leaves little time for anything else. Research indicates that a majority of entrepreneurs experience high levels of stress. However, many entrepreneurs find that some job-related stress serves as a stimulant to productivity and, at reasonable levels, is desirable.

NO HAVEN FROM RED TAPE

Poll some would-be entrepreneurs and you will find that they expect that starting a venture will free them from the reports, forms, time sheets, and red tape encountered in the corporate world. Really, this is reason to laugh. In the previous chapter we saw what a nightmare it is for entrepreneurs to prepare and update a business plan and then still be subjected to filling out the SBA's "business plan." Most of the financial and governmental institutions that you will encounter have their own set of forms. You will continuously be regurgitating much of what you have already done, in order to fit someone else's preprinted form. You can easily consume ten hours a week or more, long after start-up, filling out forms.

Banks and the SBA require a *personal* financial statement that presents detailed information about your personal assets and liabilities, income sources, and life insurance; also a listing of notes payable to banks and others including the name and address of the holder of the note, the original balance and present balance, terms of repayment and how the note is secured. You will be requested to provide information on stocks, bonds, and other securities that you own; real estate that you own including original cost, date purchased, present market value, and tax assessment value; unpaid taxes and other liabilities.

The moment you apply to institutions you will encounter a bevy of forms. The federal government, in particular, plagues small business entrepreneurs. Each year the federal government issues thousands of new regulations affecting business. The cost of federal paperwork borne by all businesses was estimated at $50.8 billion in 1984. The burden of complying with federal regulations can be crushing to small business entrepreneurs.

Studies show that the cost of federal red tape per employee in small firms is almost three times that in large firms. Though acts to stem the tide have been passed, such as the Regulatory Flexibility Act, the Paperwork Reduction Act, and the Equal Access to Justice Act, no real relief has occurred. The Regulatory Flexibility Act, for example, was designed to insure that offending agencies analyze the impact of their regulations on small business. Unfortunately, the effectiveness of the act is dependent upon small business entrepreneurs' awareness of proposed regulations and their collective ability to voice concerns to agency authorities.

While the Office of Management and Budget contends that the Paperwork Reduction Act has been effective, many small business entrepreneurs have yet to enjoy a reduction in federal government–related red tape. The Small Business Administration's Office of Advocacy has fought for years to reduce the federal paperwork-related burden faced by small business. Understandably, government regulations and red tape have been cited as one of the five most important problems facing small businesses in polls conducted by the National Federation of Independent Business of their members in each of the last ten years.

At both the 1980 and 1986 sessions of the White House Conference on Small Business, participants were eager to have legislation passed requiring government agencies that developed fiscal, monetary, legislative, and regulatory policy/practices to submit small business "economic impact statements." Such legislation would force the regulatory agencies to identify anticipated benefits and to justify the costs of federal regulatory requirements to small business. No one knows when real relief will come.

MORE RED TAPE

The accounting firm of Coopers and Lybrand offers this list of tax forms which must be filed:

- Application of Employer Identification Number (SS-4)
- Employee's Withholding Allowance Certificate (W-4)
- Wage and Tax Statement (W-2)
- Statement of Recipients of Periodic Annuities, Pensions, Retirement Pay, or IRA Payments (W-2P)
- Nonemployee Compensation (1099-MISC)

- Federal Tax Deposits:
  Withheld Income and FICA
  Unemployment Taxes
  Corporate Estimated Income Tax
- Employer's Quarterly Federal Tax Return (941)
- Employer's Annual Federal Unemployment Tax Return (940)
- Transmittal of Income and Tax Statement (W-3)

As an individual taxpayer, you are already far too familiar with the relentless grip of the IRS. As a business owner, you'll come to know and fear the IRS on an entirely different level. Federal income taxes, payroll taxes, and estate taxes as well as numerous state taxes require that a never-ending stream of forms *will be* completed in full and *will be* submitted on time.

Uncle Sam, through the IRS, is your not-so-silent partner on all major business decisions. You must continuously consider the tax implications of all major business decisions. Yet, 85 percent of all business tax returns, according to the findings of the 1986 White House Conference on Small Business, are filed through "the returns of their owners who are organized as sole proprietorships or partnerships." Thus, most entrepreneurs are operating with less than adequate knowledge of tax options. Some retain the advice of a good tax adviser; the majority try to slug it out without professional help (see Chapter 12).

If you are audited, and starting a business increases your odds dramatically, you'll easily spend weeks documenting and substantiating your prior claims. The auditors are particularly interested in detailed documentation of:

- officers' salaries
- travel and entertainment expenses
- home office deductions
- commissions, bonuses, special compensations
- anything that looks out of line for your industry

If the IRS is not enough for you, there is always OSHA—the Occupational Safety and Health Administration—with its bundle of health and safety regulations, and the corresponding state OSHA office. OSHA covers all employers engaged in business "effecting interstate commerce" and "who have one or more employees." Under this law, covered employers must furnish their employees a safe and healthful workplace. Employers must comply with numerous OSHA standards and reporting requirements as specified in the regulations. This particularly affects manufacturers, restaurant owners and food service distributors, and trucking and delivery companies.

God forbid you should set up a pension or profit sharing for your employees. The Department of Labor will be on your back regarding compliance with ERISA—Employee Retirement Income Security Act of 1974. You will be required to file:

- Form 5500—Annual return/report of Employee Benefit Plan
- Schedule A—Insurance information
- Schedule B—Actuarial information
- Schedule P—Annual return of fiduciary of Employee Benefit Trust
- Schedule SSA—Annual Registration Statement
- Form 5330—Return of initial excess taxes related to Employee Benefit Plan
- PBGC-1—Annual Premium Payment and
- Some or most of 31 other forms depending on the variables of your plan and your situation.

In addition to OSHA and ERISA, the Department of Labor also administers the Contract Work Hours and Safety Standards Acts; Davis-Bacon and related acts; Equal Employment Opportunity; Fair Labor Standards Acts; Service Contract Act; and Work Incentive Program and some sixteen others.

At the state level here's a sampling of forms you may encounter:

- Articles of incorporation
- State business and occupational tax return
- State industrial insurance report
- Federal highway use tax return

You may also be besieged by union-related reports, personal property tax affidavits, census report questionnaires, equal opportunity employee reports, etc.

As if federal and state government red tape is not burdensome enough, locally you will also have to contend with:

- Being registered to do business
- Obtaining and complying with zoning requirements
- Gathering property tax information
- Obtaining a business permit and renewals
- Obtaining local licenses and renewals
- Obtaining a local sales tax number (or an exemption)

YOUR OWN RED TAPE

If you will be employing more than a handful of employees, you will need to develop a policies and procedures handbook that includes such information as:

- The company history
- Employee privileges and benefits
- Employee responsibilities
- Employee payroll plan
- Handling expenses and deductions
- Office hours, holidays, and vacation policy
- Standards of conduct
- Performance reviews
- Use of company forms
- Reporting of absences
- Safety rules
- Probationary period
- Policy on authorized absences
  Holidays
  Vacations
  Maternity/military leave
  Disability leave
  Bereavement leave
  Jury duty
- Distribution and control of keys, security cards

- Parking and
- Some thirty-five to fifty additional items of information depending on the nature of your business, the number of employees, and how tight a ship you want to run.

If you grow large enough you will need to develop or acquire the following types of records and report forms:

- Interview summary report
- Confidential employee history report
- Wage and salary history
- Personnel card, attendance record
- Employee performance evaluation
- Payroll change notice
- Employee earning report
- Employee termination report

Employment-related lawsuits can form a large hole in your bank account. This requires that you be able to fully document and justify your handling of employees.

There is no real solution to the mountains of forms, reports, and red tape with which you tangle in owning and operating your own business. It's best to recognize in advance that red tape will be a major part of your life, and that starting a small business is certainly no haven from it. To the degree that you can, budget the time and resources that will be necessary to comply with scads of paperwork.

Maintain a central file if possible so that you or your clerical help need not frantically search the office to find essential data, code numbers, or forms that have been previously developed or assembled. By initially making a little extra effort, getting organized, setting up files, and realistically assessing the paperwork burden, you will be better positioned to handle it.

RECORD RETENTION

Getting organized will help you with the legal, tax, and management responsibilities for retaining records. The following pages list various records, and their proper retention period. Be sure to order some extra filing cabinets!

Records Retention Timetable

Legend for Authority to Dispose	Legend for Retention Period
AD—Administrative Decision	AC—Dispose After Completion of Job or Contract
ASPR—Armed Services Procurement Regulation	AE—Dispose After Expiration
CFR—Code of Federal Regulations	AF—After End of Fiscal Year
FLSA—Fair Labor Standards Act	AM—After Moving
ICC—Interstate Commerce Commission	AS—After Settlement
INS—Insurance Company Regulation	AT—Dispose After Termination
ISM—Industrial Security Manual, Attachment to DD Form 441	ATR—After Trip
	OBS—Dispose When Obsolete
*After Disposed **Normally	P—Permanent
	SUP—Dispose When Superseded
	†Govt. R&D Contracts

Type of Record	Retention Period Years	Authority
Accounting & Fiscal		
Accounts Payable Invoices	3	ASPR-STATE,FLSA
Accounts Payable Ledger	P	AD
Accounts Receivable Invoices & Ledgers	5	AD
Authorizations for Accounting	SUP	AD
Balance Sheets	P	AD
Bank Deposits	3	AD
Bank Statements	3	AD
Bonds	P	AD
Budgets	3	AD
Capital Asset Record	3*	AD
Cash Receipt Records	7	AD
Check Register	P	AD
Checks, Dividend	6	
Checks, Payroll	2	FLSA,STATE
Checks, Voucher	3	FLSA,STATE
Cost Accounting Records	5	AD
Earnings Register	3	FLSA,STATE
Entertainment, Gifts, & Gratuities	3	AD
Estimates, Projections	7	AD
Expense Reports	3	AD
Financial Statements, Certified	P	AD
Financial Statements, Periodic	2	AD
General Ledger Records	P	CFR
Labor Cost Records	3	ASPR,CFR

Type of Record	Retention Period Years	Authority
Magnetic Tape and Tab Cards	1**	
Note Register	P	AD
Payroll Registers	3	FLSA,STATE
Petty Cash Records	3	AD
P & L statements	P	AD
Salesman Commission Reports	3	AD
Travel Expense Reports	3	AD
Work Papers, Rough	2	AD
Administrative Records		
Audit Reports	10	AD
Audit Work Papers	3	AD
Classified Documents: Inventories, Reports, Receipts	10	AD
Correspondence, Executive	P	AD
Correspondence, General	5	AD
Directives from Officers	P	AD
Forms Used, File Copies	P	AD
Systems and Procedures Records	P	AD
Work Papers, Management Projects	P	AD
Communications		
Bulletins Explaining Communications	P	AD
Messenger Records	1	AD
Phone Directories	SUP	AD
Phone Installation Records	1	AD
Postage Reports, Stamp Requisitions	1 AF	AD
Postal Records, Registered Mail, & Insured Mail Logs & Meter Records	1 AF	AD,CFR
Telecommunications Copies	1	AD
Contract Administration		
Contracts, Negotiated. Bailments, Changes, Specifications, Procedures, Correspondence	P	CFR
Customer Reports	P	AD
Materials Relating to Distribution Revisions, Forms, and Format of Reports	P	AD
Work papers	OBS	AD
Corporate		
Annual Reports	P	AD
Authority to Issue Securities	P	AD
Bonds, Surety	3AE	AD
Capital Stock Ledger	P	AD

69

Type of Record	Retention Period Years	Authority
Charters, Constitutions, Bylaws	P	AD
Contracts	20AT	AD
Corporate Election Records	P	AD
Incorporation Records	P	AD
Licenses—Federal, State, Local	AT	AD
Stock Transfer & Stockholder	P	AD
Legal		
Claims and Litigation Concerning Torts and Breach of Contracts	P	AD
Laws Records—Federal, State, Local	SUP	AD
Patents and Related material	P	AD
Trademark & Copyrights	P	AD
Library, Company		
Accession Lists	P	AD
Copies of Requests for Materials	6 mos.	AD
Meeting Calendars	P	AD
Research Papers, Abstracts, Bibliographies	SUP, 6 mos. AC	AD
Manufacturing		
Bills of Material	2	AD,ASPR
Drafting Records	P	AD†
Drawings	2	AD,ASPR
Inspection Records	2	AD
Lab Test Reports	P	AD
Memos, Production	AC	AD
Product, Tooling, Design, Engineering Research, Experiment & Specs Records	20	STATUE LIMITATIONS
Production Reports	3	AD
Quality Reports	I AC	AD
Reliability Records	P	AD
Stock Issuing Records	3 AT	AD,ASPR
Tool Control	3 AT	AD,ASPR
Work Orders	3	AD
Work Status Reports	AC	AD
Office Supplies & Services		
Inventories	I AF	AD
Office Equipment Records	6 AF	AD
Requests for Services	I AF	AD
Requisitions for Supplies	I AF	AD

70

Type of Record	Retention Period Years	Authority
Personnel		
Accident Reports, Injury Claims, Settlements	30 AS	CFR,INS,STATE
Applications, Changes, & Terminations	5	AD,ASPR,CFR
Attendance Records	7	AD
Employee Activity Files	2 or SUP	AD
Employee Contracts	6 AT	AD
Fidelity Bonds	3 AT	AD
Garnishments	5	AD
Health & Safety Bulletins	P	AD
Injury Frequency Charts	P	CFR
Insurance Records, Employees	11 AT	INS
Job Descriptions	2 or SUP	CFR
Rating Cards	2 or SUP	CFR
Time Cards	3	AD
Training Manuals	P	AD
Union Agreements	3	WALSH-HEALEY ACT
Plant & Property Records		
Depreciation Schedules	P	AD
Inventory Records	P	AD
Maintenance & Repair, Building	10	AD
Maintenance & Repair, Machinery	5	AD
Plant Account Cards, Equipment	P	CFR,AD
Property Deeds	P	AD
Purchase or Lease Records of Plant Facility	P	AD
Space Allocation Records	1 AT	AD
Printing & Duplicating		
Copies Produced, Tech. Pubs., Charts	1 or OBS	AD
Film Reports	5	AD
Negatives	5	AD
Photographs	1	AD
Production Records	1 AC	AD
Procurement, Purchasing		
Acknowledgements	AC	AD
Bids, Awards	3 AT	CFR
Contracts	3 AT	AD
Exception Notices (GAO)	6	AD
Price Lists	OBS	AD
Purchase Orders, Requisitions	3 AT	CFR
Quotations	1	AD

Type of Record	Retention Period Years	Authority
Products, Services, Marketing		
Correspondence	3	AD
Credit Ratings & Classifications	7	AD
Development Studies	P	AD
Presentations & Proposals	P	AD
Price Lists, Catalogs	OBS	AD
Prospect Lines	OBS	AD
Register of Sales Order	NO VALUE	AD
Surveys	P	AD
Work Papers, Pertaining to Projects	NO VALUE	AD
Public Relations & Advertising		
Advertising Activity Reports	5	AD
Community Affairs Records	P	AD
Contracts for Advertising	3 AT	AD
Employee Activities & Presentations	P	AD
Exhibits, Releases, Handouts	2–4	AD
Internal Publications	P (1 copy)	AD
Layouts	1	AD
Manuscripts	1	AD
Photos	1	AD
Public Information Activity	7	AD
Research Presentations	P	AD
Tear-Sheets	2	AD
Security		
Classified Material Violations	P	AD
Courier Authorizations	1 mo.ATR	AD
Employee Clearance Lists	SUP	ISM
Employee Case Files	5	ISM
Fire Prevention Program	P	AD
Protection—Guards, Badge Lists, Protective Devices	5	AD
Subcontractor Clearances	2 AT	AD
Visitor Clearance	2	ISM
Taxation		
Annuity or Deferred Payment Plan	P	CFR
Depreciation Schedules	P	CFR
Dividend Register	P	CFR
Employee Withholding	4	CFR
Excise Exemption Certificates	4	CFR
Excise Reports (Manufacturing)	4	CFR
Excise Reports (Retail)	4	CFR

Type of Record	Retention Period Years	Authority
Inventory Reports	P	CFR
Tax Bills and Statements	P	AD
Tax Returns	P	AD
Traffic & Transportation		
Aircraft Operating & Maintenance	P	CFR
Bills of Lading, Waybills	2	ICC,FLSA
Employee Travel	I AF	AD
Freight Bills	3	ICC
Freight Claims	2	ICC
Household Moves	3 AM	AD
Motor Operating & Maintenance	2	AD
Rates and Tariffs	SUP	AD
Receiving Documents	2–I0	AD,CFR
Shipping & Related Documents	2–I0	AD,CFR

Revised and printed by Michael Business Machines Corp. © 1986 Reprinted with Permission

SUPPLY SHORTAGE—NOW WHAT?

Few people who start a business contemplate shortages in supply of fundamental items or raw materials. The circuit-board manufacturer doesn't envision being unable to get an adequate supply of microchips. The mason maintains good relations with a key suplier of bricks and other stone products. The oil driller isn't planning to encounter a shortage in rigging equipment and supplies.

Yet supply shortages are a fact of life for entrepreneurs. Talk to any of them and see. A supplier lets them down, a shipment is late, or worse, something in abundance becomes scarce. All major industrial corporations take great pains to ensure adequate sources of key raw materials and supplies by identifying alternative suppliers and maintaining contingency plans. The small business entrepreneur, whose time is already at a premium, and who has not experienced a previous supply disruption, may become hard pressed to find a "reliable" source of supply for some crucial item.

To avoid being caught on the short end of the stick, continuously identify and contact alternative suppliers. It is also useful and necessary to list every item that, if unavailable, would represent a hardship for your business. In a second column, list every possible substitute item that would still enable you to get the job done.

OVERCOMING YOUR OWN MISCONCEPTIONS

Two of the fastest ways to overcome your own misconceptions regarding the management of your new venture are to:

1) Get help
2) Associate with your peers

Author Ted Frost in *Where Have All the Woolly Mammoths Gone?* (Prentice-Hall, 1977) observed that executives in large corporations need to be right only 55 percent to 60 percent of the time to be regarded as successful. The entrepreneur running his/her own show cannot afford to be right such a low percentage of the time, and instead must be closer to 90 percent to 95 percent.

GETTING HELP

If getting help means hiring consultants, participating in **SBA-SCORE** (Service Corp of Retired Executives—see SCORE chapter cities list in Appendix) or ACE (Active Corp of Executives) programs, then do so. The Small Business Administration provides many excellent books, checklists, and brochures on a variety of business management topics. The SBA also has management and financial assistance programs that have been benefiting small businesses for over thirty years. The SBA, as well as local universities and private organizations, holds seminars at minimal costs, often free.

The Small Business Development Centers (SBDCs) and Small Business Institutes (SBIs), both university-based programs sponsored by the SBA, provide joint faculty/student assistance to small businesses. If you learn one new bit of information that benefits the business, then the time spent was a good investment.

Competent help is worth an $80- to $100-an-hour consultant, when the insights and advice that you receive enhance and extend your own effectiveness.

PEER GROUP ASSISTANCE

Another important way of overcoming your own management misconceptions is to associate with your peers. If you are a retail merchant, then join the local merchants' association. If there isn't one, then start one. Local groups such as the Chamber of Commerce, Board of Trade, or Rotary allow you to associate with successful entrepreneurs within your community. These are people who have experienced what you will be experiencing and can help you maintain a balanced perspective. Also, professional and trade associations, be they national or local in scope, enable you to interact directly with peers in your industry, trade, or profession.

I'm always amazed to learn that many entrepreneurs have no knowledge of the associations in their industries. Thousands of associations—covering everything from diamond cutting in New York to cheese distribution in Wisconsin—offer substantial benefits and support to the entrepreneur.

Associations supply information—mountains of it. Some of this information is especially useful in a start-up situation. For instance, if you are beginning a retail business, contact the National Retail Merchants' Association. They can supply information on start-up costs, pitfalls to avoid, and whether to lease or buy your equipment and property.

You also can get valuable *financial* information from associations. Your industry association can provide you with sample ratios or model balance sheets that will help you compare your business with others in the industry.

Associations provide a wealth of marketing information. They take surveys and polls on a regular basis to obtain current data on industry trends, market directions, and growth areas. Associations draw on the experience of their members to conduct and publish valuable studies.

Other benefits of belonging to your industry association include the right to display its plaque or logo (like the FTD winged Mercury logo displayed in most florist shops), which lends credibility to your business; access to information about legislation affecting your industry; and a newsletter containing current trends. You'll get information about upcoming conventions, workshops, and seminars. Attending association events to exchange ideas with your peers is one of the very best ways to gain information about effectively operating your business.

Begin your investigation at the library with directories such as Gale's *Encyclopedia of Associations* and *National Trade and Professional Associations* (NTPA). These contain descriptive listings including the number of members, name of the executive director, publications, conventions, etc.

Using this material, you'll find between ten and fifty associations that can help your business. The national office of an association will always be happy to give you the address and phone number of regional or local chapters.

There are also umbrella groups, such as the National Retailers' Association, and specific industry groups, like the National Shoe Retailers' Association. It's best to join at least one umbrella group and one industry specific group. For instance, you could belong to an umbrella group like the Institute of Management Consultants (those who work in all areas of consulting) and then join a specific industry group like the Independent Computer Consultants Association (those working in just that area).

Whatever your field, you can't afford to ignore associations. The dues you pay are earned back in many ways. No entrepreneur has all the resources needed to manage a business on a day-to-day basis and keep on top of the field. The learning opportunities afforded by associations, as well as the perspective gained from association membership, will give you the edge.

No amount of outside assistance will overcome all of your management problems and misconceptions. However, the entrepreneur who plays it pretty much alone is raising the odds of failure.

CHAPTER 6

The Financing Blues

Most men (and women) lead lives of quiet desperation.

—*HENRY DAVID THOREAU*

When comedian Rodney Dangerfield says, "I don't get no respect," in addition to offering an amusing comedy routine, he could also be serving as the spokesperson for the typical entrepreneur. Rodney is describing the treatment that you'll receive from bankers and others providing debt or equity capital.

One of the first shocks the start-up entrepreneur is likely to encounter when applying for loans is to learn that even if the business is incorporated, banks will still want to know if you own a home, and if so what your equity is; the value of your car; whether or not you have a life insurance policy; and other highly personal information about your personal balance sheet and income statement. The reason is simple. Until you have been in business for five years or more, your personal

77

assets will be used as collateral for any business loan that may be offered to you.

To procure financial assistance you will have to put nearly *everything that you own* on the line. You have to have faith in your proposed venture and believe to the marrow in your bones that your business will be successful. So your entrepreneurial quest takes on new meaning. No longer are you merely embarking on a new lifestyle, the pursuit of your dreams, and the ability to generate great rewards. You are also playing Russian roulette, probably with everything that you have ever saved and worked for and with your family's way of life.

THE ART OF LOANSMANSHIP

Getting a loan is an art. Much like mastering other arts, a considerable amount of discipline and preparation is necessary. Generally, the longer the payback period for a loan, the higher the risk to the bank. In order to protect itself, the bank is naturally interested in the profits that you will generate. Banks are also keenly interested in knowing if you have a guarantee from the Small Business Administration, because that greatly reduces their risk. If the loan is going to be applied specifically toward names assets, then the bank can take those assets in the event you default on the loan.

You must offer personal guarantees, and considering the length and complexity of some of the loan documents these days, you must offer them in more ways than you will ever know. The bank will take your personal assets, if it has to. If your note has been cosigned by another, his/her assets will also be under lien.

If your loan is specifically for the purchase of assets, the bank will take the first position; that is, they get the assets should you default. However, they will also take the second position on accounts receivable, inventory, or other assets. This is called an assignment, and in the case of accounts receivable, would be called "a blanket position on receivables."

In steering you past financing pitfalls, I wish to highlight three salient points:

- Preparation for outside financing must always start far in advance of the actual need.
- Cultivation of professional relations with loan officers is essential.
- Any hint of desperation is detrimental to your quest for financial assistance.

78

1. **Preparation for outside financing must always start far in advance of the actual need.** Obtaining a loan in a start-up situation requires the same kinds of skills needed to hit a moving target. The inherent lags in loan application procedures and reviews, combined with other uncertainties as to actual start-up date, distribution of funds, etc., means that even with a successful application, the actual granting of the loan may be out of sync with your plans.

Remembering Sheldon's Two-Times Law, whatever amount you are seeking should probably be increased significantly. Remembering Sheldon's Three-Times Law, you had better get started months before you thought you would have to. The inherent danger of asking for too much is that you may be rejected because the financial institution doesn't see a way to cover themselves for the full amount of the loan. The danger in asking for too little is twofold: (1) you may actually receive that amount and find it inadequate, and (2) bankers are more likely to reject applicants who ask for too little because these applicants appear to have an unrealistic view of the situation.

Which is the greater sin—asking for too much or too little? On balance, you are better off asking for too much. The banker may knock down the amount you seek and offer you a somewhat lesser figure. If you ask for too little and it is apparent to those reviewing your financial package, you have no retreat. When someone has to say to you, "Based on your situation this amount will not be adequate," you have already indicated your inability to identify your own financial needs. If this is so, the banker wonders, what are your other managerial shortcomings?

When should you start preparing materials for your loan package? The moment you are clear that you want to start a business that requires outside financial assistance. Six months to a year of advance preparation is common, and longer than that is not unusual.

Your ability to offer a detailed, credible business plan is of prime importance when seeking a loan. Specifically, when seeking debt capital you must be able to answer two basic questions:

a) How much money do you need, over what period, and how will the funds be used?
b) When and how will you pay the money back?

The most effective way to answer these questions and to provide a graphic overview of your situation is to produce both a short- and long-term cash flow analysis (see page 85).

Another aspect of your advance preparation will be to familiarize yourself with other available financing sources. On a personal basis, obviously, there are your own savings, life insurance loan programs, friends, relatives, and, not for the meek, taking out a second mortgage on your home.

Once you have been in business for a while, or have already assembled your business assets, asset-based financial measures include loans secured by accounts receivable, inventories, or fixed assets; leasing of fixed assets; or transfer of accounts receivable to another party.

Debt capital also can be raised through finance companies, SBA-guaranteed loans both with or without a commercial bank's participation, federal loans for businesses in high employment or undeveloped areas, loans from other businesses such as insurance companies, or industrial revenue bonds.

Equity capital can be raised by sale of both common and preferred stock, sale of part of the business to a venture capitalist, sale of part of the business to a small business investment corporation (SBIC), or filing with the Securities and Exchange Commission and going public. Raising equity capital requires preparing a prospectus that is much more extensive than a loan package!

2. **Cultivation of personal and professional relations with loan officers is essential.** Here is a $100,000 question. Should you take a bank loan officer to lunch? While it may seem simple, before you answer, keep in mind that 99 percent of entrepreneurs never have.

Okay, what's the answer?

The best time to get to know a loan officer is well before you ever ask for a loan. It makes good sense to get to know more than one at your primary bank, and to meet other loan officers at other banks. Many first-time entrepreneurs, upon hearing that they should invite a loan officer to lunch and discuss the highlights of a proposed plan (even if the business is already started), feel a bit sheepish.

"Why would a loan officer want to spend time with me if I am not even asking for a loan?" Particularly in this era of aggressive bank marketing, rest assured that as a potential loan recipient, creator of jobs, payer of taxes, and pillar of the community, you are someone loan officers will be interested in getting to know.

The first time entrepreneurs usually introduce themselves is the day when they walk into the bank, sit down at the desk, and begin to talk about their business. The standard line is "Everything is going well, can you lend me X amount?" (or "How much can you lend me?"). And "I need it as soon as possible." This is bad form and is not likely to win you any points. By making an immediate "I need it as soon as possible" request of a loan officer, you hardly project the image of an effective planner.

Leading financial experts agree that if you play your cards right, you can actually get favored treatment at your bank. By cultivating a relationship in advance, you can request and possibly get an interest rate that is lower than the going rate to other small businesses, and have other service costs eliminated. The better the loan officer understands your business (as typified by the more information he has on you in his file), the more effectively you'll be represented to the bank loan committee.

Loan officers are eager to develop long-term client relationships and to provide additional services such as payroll management, financial systems, or pension management. The more the loan officer is able to get to know you, the more he is able to reduce his risk and the greater the opportunity he has to build a portfolio of successful, responsible clients.

3. **The appearance of desperation is detrimental to your quest for financial assistance.** The greatest financial paradox facing the entrepreneur is to be able to obtain funds without appearing to have great need for them. If you can make requests for financial assistance as part of an overall business planning process, and not because you have to have it or else, you are way ahead of the game. One must tread a very fine line in this area.

What are some of the telltale signs that bankers look for to determine if you are in trouble? If you have too much invested in fixed assets without corresponding revenues to justify them or if you are permanently overextended—constantly operating on a shoestring—all the alarms and buzzers will go off. Loans to officers or owners for nonbusiness purposes get you a quick rejection. Similarly, if you have a pile of unpaid bills, excessive officer salaries, or heavy inventories compared to sales, the loan officer will be wary.

LINE OF CREDIT

Instead of seeking a loan each time you need a cash injection, you use a line of credit. If you have developed a sound banking relationship, obtaining a line of credit need not be that difficult. As with a traditional loan, the best time to seek this form of financing is when you don't really need it. Many of the same criterion used in judging your conventional loan application will be used in judging the line-of-credit application.

SEEKING VENTURE CAPITAL

In a start-up business situation, raising capital, either debt or equity, probably represents a great challenge. The term venture capital refers to funds that are invested in companies that are deemed to be in a "high risk" category. Many would-be entrepreneurs with whom I've dealt have unrealistic expectations regarding the efforts required to attract venture capital. Venture capitalists have been known to invest in companies: in the blueprint stage, when products or services are being conceptualized; seeking second-round financing; undergoing expansion; experiencing a turnaround—facing financial difficulties due to low profits, or bad planning; or undertaking a buyout—to finance an acquisition.

Fred Adler, a renowned venture capitalist, advises that the best way to favorably influence a venture capitalist is to offer a product or service with a competitive edge "in a field where there is recognizable opportunity for growth." It also helps to assemble a crack management team with each member a heavyweight in his field.

Adler observes that your ability to demonstrate commitment to the success of your firm, willingness to put in long, hard hours, and use of your own personal capital will be among the most significant measures of your venture capital proposal. Also be sure to indicate mistakes you have made in the past along with lessons that you have learned.

A few venture capitalists have become specialists in making investments in the $50,000 to $250,000 range. However investments under $500,000 to $1,000,000 are generally not attractive to most venture capitalists. Certain industries such as medical electronics, data processing, telecommunications, and energy conservation are more likely to pique the interest of venture capitalists than others. The reason is that only one firm in ten pays off, and that must be a big score indeed. The prevailing notion throughout the industry is that the biggest scores are derived through investing in firms with leading edge products or services in growth industries.

Besides venture capital, other sources of equity capital include: equity partnerships in which investors become limited partners (in start-up corporations that ultimately become corporations), small business investment corporations, and minority enterprise small business investment corporations. In these cases, start-up companies in traditional, nontechnical, or otherwise unexciting industries have just as good a chance of attracting capital as those in the glamour industries. However, much as when dealing with banks or venture capital firms, extensive efforts will be required to secure the funds sought.

A LOOK AT CASH FLOW PLANNING

Loan officers and investors will be keenly interested in examining your cash flow projection both for one year by month and three to five years by quarter. A well-developed cash flow projection delineates the timing and magnitude of cash needs. It is a forecast of funds a business anticipates receiving, on the one hand, and disbursing, on the other hand. Over a given time span, it plots the anticipated cash position at specific times.

Preparing a cash flow projection highlights deficiencies or excesses in cash from that necessary to efficiently operate the business. If deficiencies are revealed in the cash flow, financial plans must be altered to provide more cash, or to reduce expenditures. If excesses of cash are revealed, it might indicate excessive borrowing or idle money that could be "put to work."

The cash flow projection form provides a systematic method of recording estimates of cash receipts and expenditures, which can be compared with actual receipts and expenditures as they become known—hence the two columns, "estimate" and "actual." The entries listed on the form will not necessarily apply to every business, and some entries may not be included that would be pertinent to your specific businesses.

Hopefully, the cash position at the end of each month is adequate to meet the cash requirements for the following month. If too little, then additional cash will have to be injected or cash paid out must be reduced. If there is too much cash on hand, this money is not working for your business.

It is easy to produce a wildly inaccurate cash flow projection. The assumptions made about the projected cash inflows and outflows are as important as the actual figures themselves. Software spreadsheet programs can help simplify calculations. However, there is no substitute for the accurate input of original data.

If you have been in business for a while, previous revenue and expense data may be used in preparing projections. If you are in a start-up situation you must rely on financial source books containing industry averages, information supplied by the association or professional trade group serving your industry, plus lots of assumptions, estimates, and just plain guesswork. You can construct a crude cash flow in as little as four hours. To construct a detailed, well-researched cash flow reflectig well-founded market assumptions and resulting revenues and all expenses—cash outflows—associated with operating the business, can take anywhere from 40 to 120 hours, or more!

Here is a twelve-month cash flow projection sheet followed by an explanation of its various components.

12 MONTH CASH FLOW PROJECTION FORM

	Pre-Start-up Position		1		2		3		12		TOTAL		
YEAR MONTH											Columns 1–12		
	Estimate	Actual	Estimate	Actual	Estimate	Actual	Estimate	Actual	Estimate	Actual	Estimate	Actual	
1. CASH ON HAND (Beginning of month)													1
2. CASH RECEIPTS (a) Cash Sales	███												2 (a)
(b) Collections from Credit Accounts													(b)
(c) Loan or Other Cash injection (Specify)													(c)
3. TOTAL CASH RECEIPTS (2a + 2b + 2c = 3)													3
4. TOTAL CASH AVAILABLE (Before cash out) (1 + 3)											███		4
5. CASH PAID OUT (a) Purchases (Merchandise)													5 (a)
(b) Gross Wages (Excludes withdrawals)													(b)
(c) Payroll Expenses (Taxes, etc.)													(c)
(d) Outside Services													(d)
(e) Supplies (Office and operating)													(e)
(f) Repairs and Maintenance													(f)
(g) Advertising													(g)
(h) Car, Delivery, and Travel													(h)
(i) Accounting and Legal													(i)
(j) Rent													(j)
(k) Telephone													(k)
(l) Utilities													(l)
(m) Insurance													(m)
(n) Taxes (Real estate, etc.)													(n)
(o) Interest													(o)
(p) Other Expenses (Specify each)													(p)
(q) Miscellaneous (Unspecified)													(q)
(r) Subtotal													(r)
(s) Loan Principal Payment													(s)
(t) Capital Purchases (Specify)													(t)
(u) Other Start-up Costs	███												(u)
(v) Reserve and/or Escrow (Specify)													(v)
(w) Owner's Withdrawal													(w)
6. TOTAL CASH PAID OUT (Total 5a thru 5w)													6
7. CASH POSITION (End of month) (4 minus 6)											███		7

Here's a quick explanation of the items included on the cash flow projection form:

1. Cash On Hand
    Beginning of month—cash on hand equals cash position previous month (No. 7).

2. Cash Receipts
    (a) Cash Sales—all cash sales; omit credit sales unless cash is actually received.
    (b) Collections from credit accounts—amount to be reviewed from all credit accounts.
    (c) Loan or other cash injection—indicate here all cash injections not shown in 2(a) or 2(b) above.

3. Total Cash Receipts
    2a + 2b + 2c = 3—self-explanatory.

4. Total Cash Available
    Before cash out $(1 + 3)$—self-explanatory.

5. Cash Paid Out
    (a) Purchases—merchandise for resale or for use in product, paid for in current month.
    (b) Gross Wages (excludes withdrawals)—base pay plus overtime, if any.
    (c) Payroll Expenses (taxes, etc.)—includes paid vacations, paid sick leave, health insurance, unemployment insurance, etc. (This might equal 20% to 45% of 5(b).)
    (d) Outside Services—this could include outside labor and/or material for specialized or overflow work, including subcontracting.
    (e) Supplies (office and operating)—items purchased for use in the business, not for resale.
    (f) Repairs and Maintenance—include periodic large expenditures such as painting or decorating.
    (g) Advertising—this amount should be adequate to maintain sales volume and includes telephone book Yellow Pages cost.

(h) Car, Delivery, and Travel—if personal car is used, charge in this column, include parking.

(i) Accounting and Legal—outside services, including, for example, bookkeeping.

(j) Rent—payment for commercial space.

(k) Telephone—self-explanatory.

(l) Utilities—water, heat, light, and/or power.

(m) Insurance—coverages on business property and products, e.g., fire, liability, also workman's compensation, fidelity, etc.

(n) Taxes—real estate, plus inventory tax, sales tax, excise tax, if applicable.

(o) Interest—interest on loans (See 2c).

(p) Other Expenses (specify each)—unexpected expenditures may be included here as a safety factor.

(q) Miscellaneous (unspecified)—small expenditures for which separate accounts would not be practical.

(r) Subtotal—this subtotal indicates cash out for operating costs.

(s) Loan Principal Payment—include payment on all loans, including vehicle and equipment purchases on time payment.

(t) Capital Purchases—nonexpensed depreciable items such as equipment, building, vehicle purchases, and leasehold improvements.

(u) Other Start-up Costs—expenses incurred prior to first-month projections and paid for after the "start-up" position.

(v) Reserve and/or Escrow—example: insurance, tax, or equipment escrow to reduce impact of large periodic payments.

(w) Owner's Withdrawal—payment for owner's income tax, social security, health insurance, executive life insurance premiums, etc.

6. Total Cash Paid Out
   Total 5a thru 5w.

7. Cash Position
   End of month (4–6)—enter this amount in (1) Cash on Hand following month.

The big eight accounting firm of Peat Marwick Mitchell & Company points out that in completing a cash-flow projection many, many assumptions must be made, some of which include:

- Growth rates
- Tax rates
- Time periods required
- Production facilities
- Environmental conditions
- General economic conditions
- Contracts to be negotiated
- Competitors' actions
- Turnovers
- Capital expenditures
- Breakdowns
- Interdependence

WHAT IS YOUR CREDIT RATING?

One measure strongly considered by banks and financial institutions to whom you apply for funds, as well as other creditors and suppliers to your business, is the strength of your credit rating. Your business's credit history and financial strength are evaluated (at your request) by a credit reporter employed by a credit rating service. Your credit rating is based on the amount and quality of information gathered by interviewing you, and by consulting public records, banks and suppliers, and other sources.

It is to your advantage to cooperate fully with the rating service. This ensures that accurate up-to-date reports on you can be offered to those businesses requesting information about your company.

Suppose you have been in business for a few years, but only lately have you had trouble meeting accounts payable. What do the credit bureaus examine in determining your credit rating? Moreover, how can you keep your suppliers and creditors happy?

WHAT CREDIT BUREAUS LOOK FOR:

A thorough credit-rating service examines the following areas when making a credit evaluation:

☐ What is the character of principals, their reputation, and management ability? Are they conservative or venturesome? Do they seem intelligent? Do they have high living standards?

87

☐ Is the credit requested unreasonable or unusual for this type of business?

☐ What is the business location like, and what is the condition of the neighborhood?

☐ Is credit information readily furnished, and are answers to the point and unevasive?

☐ Do the principals have other enterprises? Do these ventures enhance the credit risk?

☐ How does the highest credit line extended to a customer compare with the present request, under current business conditions?

☐ Is business insurance adequate? Has a safety check been made to reduce the hazards of fire and other disasters?

SUPPLIERS' CREDIT CHECKS:

Many suppliers undertake their own credit evaluations. In evaluating the credit of your firm, suppliers may:

• Look for and analyze distress signals, such as partial payment being made, or notes offered in payment;

• Check in advance for guarantees or securities available, should the circumstances suggest their need;

• Examine your business hazards, personnel, sponsors, and links to other enterprises;

• Check outside mortgages, liens, or control on the management by other creditors or interested parties;

• Check to see if your operation is subject to unusual price-cutting and excessive risks, and if you are tied in with any other companies likely to affect risk;

• Obtain the facts of any bankruptcies or receiverships mentioned in your credit application;

• Check whether or not others have ever had to institute legal action for collection;

• Search public records for judgments and other liens that may not have been mentioned in the customary sources of credit information;

• Determine if there is any contest by insurance companies or underwriters about fire losses.

88

In addition, cash, accounts receivable, and inventory are investigated in detail by those checking your credit. Specific information sought includes the following.

CASH:

- Is your money on deposit with a bank that also carries your outstanding loans? In such a case the money is usually encumbered directly to the extent of that loan.
- How much of the available cash is earmarked for immediate payment of wages, dividends, bonuses, loans coming due, and purchase commitments for expansion programs?
- If there are unusually large cash balances, are there indications of inefficient use of capital?
- If there are unusually low cash balances, will assets, such as accounts receivable or inventories, have to be pledged for losses to the disadvantage of general creditors?

ACCOUNTS RECEIVABLE:

- What portion of the receivables may be classed as "good," which can be counted on for payment when due, and which are "bad"?
- Which accounts are past due and why?
- What is the credit standing of each substantial past-due account and unusually large current accounts? Do sales and past-due accounts information jibe?
- Have some accounts been sold or assigned, without being so indicated?

INVENTORY:

- Are inventories kept under control by means of accurate and detailed records?
- In consideration of seasonal changes or other factors, is the estimated liquidity of inventory sufficient?

REESTABLISHING A GOOD RATING

It is best to deal honestly with suppliers, avoiding commitments that cannot be met. Be candid about your financial strengths and weaknesses. Stated another way, when it comes to favorably influencing creditors, credit bureaus, and suppliers, honesty is the best policy. After being in business for at least a year or two, if the relationship with suppliers has been straightforward, your suppliers can be used as valuable sources of short-term financing via the extension of trade credit.

The best way to reestablish a good credit with suppliers is to enclose a personal, detailed letter to each with the next payment due. The letter should explain the reasons for slow payment in the past, other difficulties, and offer a brief synopsis of present operations. It should also thank the supplier for exhibiting patience (and support, if applicable) with the assurance that every effort is being made and will continue to be made toward the development of a solid working relationship.

If you are wary of all the financial preparations and planning discussed thus far and it seems like a lot of work, it is.

If you are a woman or a member of a minority group, even in the supposedly enlightened climate of the late eighties, you will find the deck continues to be stacked against you. Despite the passage of the Equal Credit Opportunity Act many delegates for the 1986 White House Conference on Small Business were concerned that the dollar volume of loans made to minority-owned and woman-owned businesses has not been increasing at a significant pace.

SECOND-ROUND FINANCING IS EVEN HARDER

Many entrepreneurs have learned the hard way that obtaining second-round financing from a bank is much more difficult than first round. This is an important statement and one that must not be dismissed lightly. You break your back to get your first loan to make a go of a business in the early years. The irony of financing is that as revenue is increasing and the business is about to expand, it becomes most difficult to portray the business in a favorable light. Why is this so?

With increased revenues, certain expenditures tend to increase— for marketing, inventory, labor, and other variable costs such as commissions, delivery, and shipping.

90

Since these expenditures are made prior to the actual receipt of revenue, financial statements of the business are likely to reflect a weakened position. Cash-flow projections may indicate an improved cash position several months in the future, with large cash deficits leading up to those months. The sad truth is that many businesses have failed because of lack of second-round financing, just at that point *at which they were about to achieve rapid growth.*

NO RESPECT, ROUND TWO

Martin T. was the head of a four-year-old advertising and public relations firm in Indianapolis. Martin started the business entirely on his own funds. After one year he sought a $12,000 loan to buy more equipment and offer a greater level of professional service. Martin got the loan at the same bank where he had maintained a personal savings account and a business checking account.

At the start of his third year, Martin had three times as many employees as a year before. Understandably his payroll was getting quite large. At the same time, Martin was doing a booming business and the size of his accounts receivable was inching up steadily. Martin had been in pursuit of two major clients, one for more than a year. Then in the same week he landed both of them!

With such fortune also came new challenges. Martin would have to increase his staff by 50 percent. Also, he would have to acquire several pieces of equipment to handle the increase in business. Given all that was occurring, Martin made the decision to move into larger quarters. The new quarters carried a monthly rent 35 percent higher than he was presently paying.

Always an excellent planner, and having maintained excellent relationships with his bank over the years, Martin took his loan officer to lunch one afternoon. Martin requested a loan of $75,000 and a doubling of his line of credit. Martin had come armed with the necessary financial projections and supporting information the loan officer needed to see. They both left the lunch table that afternoon in good spirits, and in full understanding and agreement with each other's position.

Martin knew that the loan was not definite until it was actually approved. Still, in order to proceed with his plans, he had to make some basic assumptions. Over the next two weeks Martin charted the next twelve to eighteen months for his firm.

One afternoon when he was busy working on something else, the loan officer called to tell him that the committee had decided against granting the loan. The words had only partially sunk in. Martin asked "What?" The loan officer commiserated. She was as surprised as Martin that the request was rejected. Martin pressed to find why he'd been rejected but couldn't get a sufficient explanation.

Having time to reflect on what had occurred, Martin was stunned and embittered. For years he had been a faithful bank patron, had honored all loan commitments, and had kept his banker abreast of his progress on a regular basis. He was no stranger to the bank. His business was a success, and everyone involved with it knew it.

By any measure he could determine, his loan request was reasonable. What real risk did the bank have honoring his loan request? He could see none.

All this mental chatter was getting him nowhere. His bank had left him out in the cold. Martin was beset with the problem of having to find a new bank, establish a new relationship, and most important, procure the desired funds. He accepted this setback because he had no other choice.

In discussion with fellow business owners he learned that many had experienced the same type of letdown. Exchanging information with others on which banks to contact, Martin was finally able to find a bank and a loan officer who was comfortable working with his type of business. Ultimately, Martin got the loan, fourteen weeks after his initial quest.

His expansion plan temporarily thwarted, Martin muddled through much as he had done in the past. Perhaps the long-term effects on his business will be negligible. But Martin was the exception. This story could have ended, and most often does, with the entrepreneur experiencing great difficulty in finding a new bank and having to wait an inordinate amount of time to receive the requested funds, if ever.

Poetic justice would dictate that the bank owes an extra measure of consideration to longstanding clients, and at least an explanation of loan rejections. This is simply not the case. Bank priorities change, bank personnel change, and the amount of funds available for making loans fluctuates. At any point along the trail, your application may be rejected based on circumstances that have less to do with the size and nature of your request than the prevailing environment.

Is there a solution to becoming a victim of the vicissitudes of the loan committee? There are some things that can be done. First, select your bank carefully. Examine them just as carefully as they examine you. Find out who is on the board, who their officers are, the size of their assets, and the reputation they have in the community. What do they charge compared to other banks, what types of programs are available, and what is their relationship to other entrepreneurs in your line of business?

Second, maintain a network of communication with other entrepreneurs and join those civic and community associations in which representatives from several banks are members. Never take your present bank for granted—they may let you down at any moment. This is not being defensive, just realistic.

Finally, don't hold loan officers in awe. They are in business to make a profit just like you. If they don't make loans, they don't make profits. A good loan officer needs to find entrepreneurs running viable businesses as much as those entrepreneurs need to find a good loan officer.

LOW PERSONAL EARNINGS

Through it all, there is a law to which entrepreneurs seeking outside financing must adhere. You are expected to draw a modest to medium salary your first several years in business. No loan officer or investor wants to give you a raise over what you earned in your previous position. Your earnings can suffer a while. Perhaps you should get less than you received at your last salaried position. The intended message seems to be: "Okay, we will give you the loan (or will invest in the business) but you are going to have to work like a dog for it. You can demonstrate your undying commitment by working for scraps."

If you don't believe this, check it out. I have asked entrepreneurs how much they thought they should be paid for their first, second, and third years in business. Responses are modestly healthy. Some say $40,000, some say $50,000, some say $75,000. I say good luck.

Even if a loan officer lets you have a $40,000 salary based on your cash flow projection, how much are you really earning? If it were $40,000 for a forty-hour week or forty-five hour week, that's one thing. However, for a fifty-four hour week, the minimum you will probably average, you are effectively working at the same rate as someone who makes $29,630 for a forty-hour week. If you are a proprietor, you have to subtract the cost of insurance and benefits. These cannot be expensed on the company books.

Around the third or fourth month you may have to miss a pay check here and there. Everyone else gets paid before you. By year's end, you may find that you are working for about $10/hour. That was fine in 1970, but today $10/hour will put you below the earnings of urban area executive secretaries and word processors.

In Chapter 8 we will further examine the phenomenon of why the amount of capital you think you will need is never enough.

CHAPTER 7

Personnel Problems

So much of what we call management consists in making it difficult for people to work.

—PETER DRUCKER

The people you employ will let you down. Once you can accept this, you'll have a better perspective with which to start a business.

Whether your business will employ only a handful or several dozen employees, you'll be involved in time-consuming personnel issues—recruiting, hiring, retaining, evaluating, compensation, and handling myriad other factors that involve dealing with the people who staff the organization. Personnel problems will occur in all these areas—tough issues that range from how to find and attract the most qualified people to how to keep them productive and effective. These problems tend to be amplified among small and/or new businesses, and many an entrepreneur has been stymied by the inability to successfully resolve them.

Personnel problems require more energy, patience, and savvy than the typical entrepreneur ever anticipates at the outset.

EMPLOYEE SITUATION FOR SMALL BUSINESS

The 1986 report of the White House Conference on Small Business describes the employee situation for small business as stable in coming years, with a somewhat older work force evolving as the baby boom generation ages. Although the number of workers who are college graduates is on the increase, so too is the number of high school dropouts.

The report noted that small businesses hire and train many more employees than do large businesses, accounting for the initial work experience and on-the-job training of two-thirds of all workers in the United States. A profile of U.S. employees shows that more women, older people, and young people are hired by small firms than by large companies, as are more high school dropouts and fewer college graduates.

Personnel problems for new businesses start early—at the point of attracting qualified personnel. Large businesses have the advantage of offering greater opportunities for growth and advancement, more extensive benefit plans, higher pay, and more sophisticated means for dealing with personnel problems as they occur. Larger firms are also more in a position to absorb certain personnel problems—from low productivity to high turnover—than are small firms, which often survive or die depending on the fullest possible utilization of each employee.

Small firms also meet more obstacles in retaining staff. Unfortunately, these problems pertain especially to the best of the personnel, where initial training has been provided within the firm itself. The White House Conference on Small Business found that the average small business loses 15 to 20 percent of its work force *each year* to larger firms—a major loss when you consider that these workers were initially trained by an entrepreneur with limited resources. Marginal employees may seem satisfied to stay forever, but the real contributors are well aware of opportunities elsewhere.

THE HAIR-RAISING SCREENING PROCESS

The task involved in hiring employees includes sifting out those who are unsuitable. Big companies use sophisticated means, such as assessment centers and validated tests, to enhance their chances of getting the right person in the right job. Small business entrepreneurs generally rely on a simple interview or two, and a couple of quick reference checks. The better the position available appears to potential applicants—in terms of pay, opportunity, responsibility, etc.—the more it will attract unqualified applicants, who tend to exaggerate their credentials and abilities. All of which means the entrepreneur is prone to make more mistakes in hiring.

Another common pitfall in hiring is focusing on something that you value, while failing to achieve a balanced perspective in assessing candidates. John Saylor is typical of entrepreneurs who cause themselves problems by getting carried away with just one aspect of a candidate's résumé. In his case, it was the Ivy League graduates who caught his eye.

Saylor made a point of hiring newly graduated Ivy Leaguers and was particularly impressed with their ability to espouse the latest management techniques and theories. He lavishly praised these new recruits to existing staff, holding them up as examples of what everyone should be doing. This stirred up resentment among company veterans.

Typically, however, Saylor's infatuation with his latest recruit wore off within a matter of months. Nobody could live up to his over-inflated expectations, and disappointment soon set in on both the side of the employer and the employee. Most new recruits left politely within a year when they realized they were no longer being singled out for the plum assignments or consulted for ideas and opinions. Thus, Saylor was constantly faced with the very activity he managed poorly—recruitment and hiring.

If you place a classified advertisement, expect to spend quite a while sifting through résumés once the word gets out. Phony résumés abound— with misstatements ranging from lies about educational degrees to exaggerations about work responsibilities. Some experts estimate that nearly 80 percent of all résumés contain at least some misleading information, generally in the area of employment history. Verifying résumé information is costly and time-consuming and sometimes nearly impossible. Common areas of résumé misrepresentation include:

1. **Filling employment gaps.** Many job candidates have gaps of months or years when they were unemployed or employed in jobs that they wouldn't wish to mention. This is especially true of those who were fired or feel they could not receive a favorable reference. These gaps may show up on résumés or applicants may simply stretch out the

time of other positions in order to fill the gaps. If a résumé gives work history information with job dates that include years, rather than specific months, of job beginnings and ends, such stretching is easy. Also feigned self-employment is often used as a way to fill a job gap. Verifying the information to check possible gaps is a tedious, difficult task for the employer.

2. **College credits.** It is amazing how easy it has become for applicants to credit themselves with college experiences they never had—including institutions they never attended, courses of study they never pursued, and degrees they never earned. This bit of fictional résumé writing among job applicants is generally risk-free because most employers are unlikely to question such a basic assertion. If the college credentials on a résumé are really impressive, it's easy to believe that they represent the truth rather than search out falsehoods.

You can save yourself time—and mistakes—by simply asking the candidate for a transcript from the institution(s) listed on the résumé. Or ask for faculty references from that institution. Many entrepreneurs don't do this.

When a job applicant attends a course or a summer program at a prestigious university, he/she may inflate the experience into something closer to an earned degree. One individual I know received a B.S. and an M.B.A. from a small obscure college in the Midwest. Later, he attended a short-term executive development program from a major, highly regarded university in the Northeast. Thereafter, he presented his educational background to potential employers in a way that would lead most people to believe his M.B.A. was from the major northeastern university.

3. **Inflated accomplishments.** Some résumés are likely to cross your desk with lists of specific accomplishments that read like:

> *"Saved the company thousands of dollars . . ."*
> *"Achieved 200 percent over quota . . ."*
> *"Substantially increased the market share . . ."*

Verify such claims by asking for specific dollar amounts or percentages, to guard against hiring someone on the basis of his/her puffery. By asking questions about exactly how much, who was involved, when and how this occurred, you'll have a fair chance spotting exaggeration and misrepresentation.

CHECKING REFERENCES

When you check references, you'll have to do so by telephone, even though this may mean calling back several times or waiting days for a busy person to return your call. More information can be obtained in a shorter time over the phone, and the voice cues you get (i.e., pauses, hemming and hawing) can be extremely helpful. Since many people find it difficult to present negative comments on paper, their written response to you is likely to be generally laudatory.

It is time consuming to prepare yourself for a reference call, but it is a *must*. First, you'll have to review the candidate's résumé and any interview notes you have made. You must consider the relationship of the candidate to the person you are calling. And you'll need to prepare or refer to a written list of questions to ask. Here are the types of questions you should be asking:

1) What are the exact dates of the applicant's employment with your organization/company/department/firm?
2) What were the applicant's initial responsibilities when starting work with you?
3) What were the applicant's last job responsibilities?
4) What level of supervision did the applicant require?
5) Did the applicant prefer to work as part of a team or on his/her own?
6) What was the applicant's record of attendance?
7) Can you cite three to five examples of the applicant's strengths?
8) Can you cite three to five examples of the applicant's weaknesses?
9) Does the applicant possess quick learning ability? If not, adequate learning ability?
10) What is the applicant's record compared to others, i.e., peers, co-workers, those with similar duties or responsibilities?
11) Based on your knowledge, why did the applicant depart (or why is the applicant departing) from your organization?
12) How did you replace the applicant upon his/her departure?
13) What was the final compensation earned by the applicant in your organization?
14) Given your experience with the applicant and in considering the job requirements, would you rehire the applicant?

99

Even major corporations, such as Mobil, Pfizer, and Ford, that use recruiting specialists or mount major college recruitment campaigns find that these efforts do not necessarily guarantee the desired results. Eli Ginzberg, professor at the Columbia University Graduate School of Business, maintains that there really is no sure way to identify the right employee in advance, and even the most sophisticated executive screening process can't help.

He believes that only on-the-job experience can tell you whether a new employee is right for you. He notes, "There's nothing in a young person's college career that will tell you about the things the company really wants to know about him. The relationship between what he can do and what he will do in a company once he joins is only remotely related to college grades."

Ginzberg suggests that you should pay more attention to the early work assignments you give to new employees offering them meaningful (when possible) and difficult tasks, and assessing how they accomplish these. If they perform well, you will know more about their abilities and drives than you could ever know during the recruitment process. "Avoid getting them started with the dull, dreary assignments that are dead-ended," he emphasizes. "Save those jobs for the dull and dreary dead-ended people who really enjoy that work."

Is there anything that can guide the selection process and help avoid the problem of discovering hiring errors after a new employee is already on the job? Probably not, but Ginzberg offers this advice: "Avoid hiring those at the very bottom of the class (they are usually lazy) and those at the very top (they are often too bright and independent)."

DON'T BE SO QUICK TO HIRE

When hiring, it is tempting to be guided by your intuition and your first impressions by simply hiring a "good" candidate on the spot. The résumé is impressive, and you click with the applicant during the interview, so why not just tell him/her he's hired?

Even when a seemingly "right" employee is found, trouble could occur in the early months of the job when any one of the following circumstances is present:

- A person is hired for less compensation than he or she previously achieved.

- A new hire does not have supervisory responsibilities but previously did.
- The position does not really represent forward movement for the new employee.
- A clear, mutual understanding of job responsibilities was never established.

These four "built-in turnover factors" provide a good troubleshooting checklist for hiring. For example, you may be delighted to get a talented person for less pay and less responsibility than that person previously commanded. However, it is essential to determine why this individual is accepting this employment. The answer may be that he/she is simply taking a position to provide ready cash while continuing to look for something more appropriate. Or perhaps the new employee just wanted a change, a smaller company, more flexible hours, or other items you may be offering that don't relate to pay and responsibility. Still, he/she will likely eventually miss the financial rewards and responsibilities of the previous job, and may become disillusioned and dissatisfied very quickly.

Likewise, if the position does not represent a new career or upward movement, you may be hiring someone who simply plans to "coast" on the job until retirement. A person who doesn't care much about his or her own career also might not care much about your company and the job he/she holds with it.

Relating to the final two factors on the list above, remember that you'll need to spend time orienting a new employee to the job. Even employees who love autonomy need initial training or instruction on how their jobs fit into the rest of the company and what exactly is expected of them. Later, they may be able to work with little or no "hand holding," but in the beginning they will become frustrated if they are not provided with a clear road map of their responsibilities.

Similarly, employees leave jobs when their work turns out to be something different from what they expected. Expectations, responsibilities, and duties need to be clarified at the outset—beginning with the first interview—and clarified again as soon as the employee comes on the job. Written job descriptions are essential. However, they only work if they accurately reflect the level of performance and exact duties that will be expected.

AND THAT'S ONLY THE BEGINNING

Once you've committed the necessary time and energy to the hiring process, you can rest easy and watch the successful new employees dedicate themselves to the good of your company. Right? Wrong!

James Forest was owner and chief executive officer of a small cabinet-making firm in Pennsylvania. He prided himself on his ability to select bright, energetic people—both in craftsmanship and supervisory capacities. Each time a job opening developed, he carefully screened candidates, called references, and held lengthy interviews. He had others in the firm interview the top candidates to gain a well-rounded set of impressions. By the time a job offer was made, Forest was convinced of the excellent match between the new hire and his company.

Nevertheless, in many cases, it only took a few months for many of Forest's "can't miss" employees to falter in their performance or to begin looking for new jobs. When a management consultant took a look at the situation, he noticed that Forest's enthusiasm about the new employees' abilities was often at the root of the problem.

Since Forest knew they were just right, he gave them little training or instruction. New employees were not told how much responsibility they had, but were left to "test the waters" themselves. In most cases, this meant they hung back and waited to be told, eventually getting frustrated. It took a long time to feel like a contributing member of the company. They were bright and talented, but were given little direction about how they could bring their talents to bear on the job. When they became confused about how much initiative to take, they tended to perform less effectively or seek other employment.

As the new employee becomes a veteran, the retention difficulties don't go away—they just change a bit. You will need to establish an objective and equitable system for how people are evaluated and promoted. Your best employees will leave if they feel they are becoming dead-ended in their opportunities for growth and advancement, and they will certainly depart if they suspect that your evaluation and advancement system is unfair or subjective.

In many small companies, the best employees leave because they sense that they can never break through to the very top. Ginzberg says, "Top management—usually the entrepreneur—is loath to give up any power. And by failing to give up power, to pass on responsibility, they effectively stalemate upcoming people." The most valuable employees thrive when given responsibility and authority—exactly what entrepreneurs often are reluctant to offer.

THE EMPLOYEE WHO KNOWS MORE THAN YOU

You may have to rely on the expertise of employees with specialized knowledge that goes well beyond your grasp. This is increasingly so in the area of data processing, a fast-changing, highly technical function that requires able specialists. But it also can occur when a company requires specialized abilities in areas like engineering, chemistry, statistical analysis, drafting, laboratory testing, and many other functions.

You may find it uncomfortable to depend on people who are doing things you don't altogether understand. And managing these employees in a way that maximizes their effectiveness is tricky. It is tempting to give them either too long or too short a leash.

Consider the case of Sam Hiseman, hired by a civil engineering firm to initiate and oversee the firm's use of computer graphics. His supervisor, John Atree, had little knowledge of data processing and was quite surprised at how "different" Hiseman was from other employees. He rarely interacted with his supervisor or others, and seemed aloof and distant as he kept to his computer terminal.

Sometimes Sam seemed to spend precious time daydreaming, just staring into space while seated at the terminal. Since Atree had no idea how long it should take his new computer specialist to perform various tasks, he simply had to trust that work was being done efficiently—but sometimes he wondered. John assumed everything involving computers should happen fast.

After many attempts, and some failures, at evolving a satisfactory working relationship, Atree and Hiseman finally did manage to develop a process that resulted in effective work and effective supervision within the bounds of the highly specialized work being performed. When handling employees with specialized knowledge you'll have to establish some basic ground rules.

- The employee must be oriented to the company in a way that allows an understanding of how his/her work fits in with company goals and with ongoing and future projects.
- The employee should be required to attend meetings, participate on task forces, give briefings, etc., to the same degree as any other employee at that level.

- The entrepreneur and/or supervisor and the employee need to work out specific goals and objectives together for work to be performed and for evaluative criteria.

- Any information needed by the supervisor of a technical, specialized nature should be accompanied by narrative documentation from the employee in a format that can be understood by the supervisor.

It is a mistake for you to avoid supervising a technical specialist and simply decide, "She knows what she's doing." There are experts in any given field who can "sound good" but really are not dedicated to getting the job done in an effective or efficient manner. Only good supervision can determine whether such an employee is a valuable contributor to the company.

PEAKS AND VALLEYS

Your most productive employees are only human and will vary in their work habits from time to time. Your challenge will be to manage them through the peaks and valleys. Typically, new college graduates seem to mope through the summer. Their performance slides off because they just haven't gotten used to the idea that summer no longer means vacation time. Other employees have a hard time getting through the Christmas holidays without a change in work behavior. Still others are greatly affected by changes in the weather. Here is what you'll have to contend with in a typical year:

January and February

A week or two after the holidays, during the dead of winter, many employees begin to get depressed. Fewer daylight hours mean that many staff members commute to and/or from the office in the dark. This gives them the feeling that they're "missing the day."

A few blizzards of snow storms in February, rough traveling, and the feeling of being stranded contribute to people's depression. It is during this time, however, that many employees display great productivity, because they look to their jobs as a source of activity and fulfillment.

March and April

In most parts of the country, spring still has not arrived in March. March has variable weather: a warm day here, a snow storm the next, howling winds or rains another day. This pattern actually can be more disruptive than January and February.

By the end of March, daylight hours increase. Spirits begin to pick up. Then, April's sporadic days of sunshine boost energy levels. By the end of April and heading into May, many employees are super-charged, maintaining one of their greatest motivation periods of the year.

May and June

As days of sparkling sunshine ensue, staff's rising energy levels, which had been directed toward their jobs, often become refocused on "spring clean-up" and outdoor activities. Many entrepreneurs notice their staff's decline in output as soon as the flowers bloom, or when the first beach weekend occurs.

The reduction of attention span and overall productivity decline remain for several weeks in mid-May and throughout June. Then, just when meeting production schedules seems hopeless, the sunshine-filled days become the standard, and employees adjust to and accept summer. They renew their efforts on the job and, often, the humidity makes everyone quite happy to be busily at work in the air-conditioned office, shop, or plant.

July and August

Surprisingly, the deep summer months do not represent the pits of productivity that supervisors may fear. Sure, many people take their vacations during this time, which can disrupt operations. But July and the dead of August can indeed be times of reasonable staff output.

The end of August, however, is a different story. Many employees seem to be in a holding pattern of rather low productivity, which is miraculously cured immediately after Labor Day.

September through mid-November

As the kids go back to school, the humidity breaks up, and a chill returns to the night air, employees once again become highly energized. The time from just after Labor Day through mid-November often represents the period of greatest productivity.

This is a good time to give staff new challenges and undertake major projects. The federal government and many corporations begin their fiscal year October 1. Fall—and spring—is a time of new hiring. Many entrepreneurs wish that autumn lasted all year long.

Mid-November through December

This six- to seven-week end-of-the-year period is broken up by holidays, longer weekends, and vacation time. However, leading up to Thanksgiving, many employees continue great accomplishment. And, following Thanksgiving vacation through mid-December, workers may stay motivated.

Approaching Christmas, however, you will readily notice a drop in output, as staff members focus attention on shopping or travel. A slew of parties and activities throughout December can contribute to a general sluggishness in effort. The turkey, wine, cookies, and eggnog tend to leave everyone a little heavier, a little slower, and a little less productive. Many managers write off the last half of December. This is a good time, however, to instill company spirit and get organized.

EMPLOYEE TIME WASTING CAN KILL YOU

After ten years as a building contractor, Frank Owen decided to start his own development and construction firm. Although he planned to keep his company small, he realized he needed quite a few full-time employees, including two secretaries, a bookkeeper, a field supervisor, and a team of laborers. As the business grew, he hired even more employees to cover as many as six construction projects at once.

As his number of employees grew, Owen noticed that their productivity seemed to drop, commenting: "When we were just starting up, it was one big family pulling together. Everyone really worked. But as we added more people we seemed to add more ways to avoid working. I've seen everything from chatting with friends and relatives on the company phone to taking hour-long coffee breaks. And I can't spend my time looking over everyone's shoulders to make sure they don't waste time. I have enough to do just managing my business; I can't be a policeman too."

What Owen was experiencing is typical of small growing companies, much as in large ones. Employees will find ways to waste time. It is a problem that grows as your company grows—time wasting among some seems to beget more time wasting among others. When you add up the costs in terms of real hours lost, you'll be shocked at the money your company is losing. Some favorite employee time-wasting tactics you'll need to be alert to include:

Coasting until check-out time

Many employees simply quit work when possible, fifteen to thirty minutes before closing time. Others stay on the job, but mentally quit by spending those last segments of the day doodling or conversing with others. This also occurs before lunch hour. The costs mount quickly. If sixteen employees earning an average of $13.50 per hour coast for an average of forty-five minutes per day, you can figure your firm will lose over $40,000 a year (with employee benefits and other costs added to salary costs). Only your own diligence can dissuade this kind of coasting, and then that takes a toll on you.

Organizing and reorganizing

You want your employees to be organized about their workplace and work habits. Yet, you'll find many who use this as a favorite time waster by unnecessarily shuffling and reshuffling papers on desks, files, and shelves. Much of this time-wasting technique takes place during "coasting time" at the end of the day or before lunch. As a general rule, an employee who can find needed information from a file or desk within a minute is sufficiently organized. Any further time spent in organizing and reorganizing is generally a sign of time wasting.

Carefully reading junk mail

Any employee who has been with an organization for more than three months is a target for junk mail, both personal and professional. The longer the employee is in one place, the more mailing lists he/she lands on. Productive employees discard junk mail immediately without even opening most of it. Others, however, use junk mail as a prop in their time-wasting activities. They take delight in opening every piece, thoroughly perusing the contents, and even filling out catalogue order forms and contest entries while at the office. Even when you instruct the person responsible for distributing mail to weed out the junk, many employees will simply find a substitute for time wasting.

107

Copy catting

Another favorite tool of the determined time waster is the office copying machine. By copying everything possible—most unnecessarily—an employee can actually look busy while wasting time. Furthermore, the copy machine may be in a nice spot—either providing the privacy some employees crave or the central location that allows access to colleagues. A really active copy cat doesn't just stop with copying office documents, but moves on to recipes, personal tax forms, a daughter's grade school report card, cartoon strips, and myriad other items. Thus, the copy cat manages to cost the company money not only in his or her own time wasted but in the cost of running the machine. Copy control devices are available, but excess copy costs continue regardless.

On the move

Some employees just can't seem to stay in one place long enough to get their jobs done. Their time wasting takes the look of movement—activity that may even look productive until a second glance. The employee who undertakes this time-wasting device can be seen walking briskly to the copier room, walking back to the mail pickup, walking over to an associate's desk, striding to the restroom, getting up for another drink from the water fountain, and even emptying wastebaskets and straightening Venetian blinds.

This individual typically looks very efficient, and some of the activity might even involve seemingly necessary actions like pulling files or sharpening pencils. But generally it amounts to a lot of running around in circles.

Taking two lunch breaks

This time-waster is particularly practiced in outdoor or factory settings where employees have plenty of room to maneuver. It occurs when an employee manages to munch a sandwich and sip a soda before the lunch hour—taking anywhere from ten to thirty minutes to do so. Then, at lunch hour, the employee takes off again—using up every minute of the lunch hour.

Paycheck activity

The activity surrounding the arrival of paychecks is another time-honored time-waster. It starts with your staff organizing their desks to wait for the arrival of the paycheck or chatting with one another about whether the checks will be early or late this time. Then, the next coffee break constitutes a mad dash to the bank, with employees mumbling about long lines as they return fifteen minutes late from the break.

While the above list of time-wasters is by no means comprehensive, it does indicate how easily such counterproductive activities can flourish. Obviously, close supervision and jobs that really stimulate employee productivity are essential in helping to alleviate the situation. If you and your company cannot provide these on an ongoing basis, you'll quickly find out that the real costs of time wasting can put you out of business.

The problem is universal to business. According to a 1982 study by employment specialist Robert Half, "Employees' deliberate waste of on-the-job time cost American business over $125 billion a year, triple the cost of shoplifting, fraud, and other crimes."

GET TOUGH ON MOONLIGHTING

Moonlighting on the job is another source of time wasting, and employees have been known to run whole companies from their desks at their primary place of employment. Maybe you have. While most employers appreciate drive and initiative in an employee, they want it directed to the job at hand, not to a second job or entrepreneurial activity. Moonlighting can mean employees spending paid time doing other things on the job *and* it can mean employees working at home with little energy left during their paid hours at your company.

For example, if Mary Smith is scheduled to work forty hours a week, but manages to sneak in an hour each day of that time to her own mail-order craft business, she only works thirty-five hours a week but is paid for forty. The thirty-five hours she puts in each week may not be very productive because she is up late at night packaging orders at home in her basement. You lose both real hours and normal productivity during the hours that are worked.

Many moonlighting individuals simply can't resist using your typewriters, telephone, and copy machine for their moonlighting endeavors.

Although one moonlighting employee may not inspire others to take a second job, there is a contagious factor in the general time wasting that occurs. Other employees may feel, "If Mary can use the phone to call a client, I can use it to call my mother." The moonlighting activity is unfair to other employees who may have to make up for work left undone, and many of them will find their own time-wasters in an attempt to make the situation more equitable.

As with other time-wasters, it takes time and good supervision to guard against moonlighting. According to Thomas P. Ference, Ph.D., also at Columbia University's Graduate School of Business, "Moonlighting is a natural and reasonable response to the complexity of employment and should not be swept under the table. It should be dealt with professionally like any other aspect of business."

You will have to develop a written policy that states the conditions under which your company approves or disapproves of moonlighting. It must include a statement pertaining to the use of employee on-the-job time and company resources, and should clarify expectations about on-the-job productivity and conflicts of interest.

THE HIGH COST OF TARDINESS AND ABSENTEEISM

Two of the most frequent and annoying personnel problems are tardiness and absenteeism. Employees can be highly creative in inventing excuses for not being at work or not being at work on time—excuses developed with an eye toward being granted administrative leave, sick leave, or any other kind of leave that involves still managing to get paid while being off the job.

Research on absenteeism reveals that patterns are fairly predictable, many of them relating to the following observations:

- Emotional factors are involved in about 25 percent of all employee absences.
- Unskilled and semiskilled workers are absent more than are skilled workers.
- A relatively small segment of the work force is responsible for most absenteeism.
- About 30 percent of employees are practically never absent from work.
- Long-service, older employees are absent less than the under 25 age group.
- Approximately 50 percent of all short (one- or two-day) absences precedes or follows legitimate time off for weekends or holidays.

- Absenteeism increases with prolonged overtime and extended work weeks.

- There is a high correlation between employee "illness" and major sports events.

Use of drugs and their ill effects are a cause for absenteeism on the part of an increasing number of people in the work force.

Employees are most apt to be absent *when you need them the most!* I've witnessed this phenomenon countless times. When employees are absent, your other employees and you have to work harder to make up for them. This, naturally, leads to frustration and dissatisfaction among your best workers—a typical by-product of absenteeism.

Entrepreneurs report that they have "tried everything" to curb absenteeism, but to no avail. Warnings seem to simply generate more creative excuses, and even lost pay may not effect the employee who feels it is his or her right to be away from work when it best suits.

The best policies in this area seem to be those that are clear and in writing, and very strict—allowing for no excuses or second chances. They generally start with verbal warnings. This occasion should also be used to ascertain any circumstances that may be at the root of absences. Verbal warnings that go unheeded need to be followed by a written notice about absenteeism—preferably that only two unexcused absences will be tolerated before action is taken.

From there, the policy needs to accommodate escalation to suspension and discharge. Such a policy needs to be used objectively and without exception if it is to have the desired effort of eliminating unnecessary absences.

EMPLOYEE THEFT—MORE COMMON THAN YOU THINK

There are many kinds of dishonesty that happen every day in companies throughout the country—from stealing office supplies to lying about hours spent on the job. Whether it represents small lies or great embezzlements, such employee dishonesty can eat into your profit margin and endanger your ability to stay in business.

Employee dishonesty can spread beyond the theft of time to the theft of real goods—be it money acquired through padded expense accounts or actual items stolen from the workplace. A Department of Justice study, "Thefts by Employees in Work Organizations," found that approximately $10 billion annually is lost by American companies to employee pilferage. Even if yours is not a retail store with inventory at risk, you have plenty that can be stolen ranging from office supplies to long distance phone calls.

Because they are "insiders," employees quickly learn how to get around problems posed by security devices or spot checks. Some areas in which you can spot employee dishonesty include:

- Mismatched inventory records and physical evidence
- Missing control documents
- Unexplained rise in consumption of supplies
- Unexplained rise in refunds or credits
- Alterations, erasures, and penciled changes on various control documents
- Missing files
- "New" inventory cartons with some items missing
- Supplies and/or inventories found elsewhere than their usual position

The issue of theft can become more problematic the more you try to stop it. In seeking to catch the culprit who is stealing supplies, you'll need to assume that everyone is guilty at first. That means that morale can take a nose dive.

Worse are cases where the entrepreneur is reluctant to prosecute fraud and theft to its fullest. The hope is that it's just a one-time occurrence by an otherwise productive worker. This is a major mistake—the situation is not likely to reverse itself.

You'll have to develop and follow several rules for avoiding and dealing with such theft, such as 1) creating an environment of high ethics, where honesty is rewarded and dishonesty is not tolerated, 2) looking for signs of theft and fraud at all times, 3) dealing swiftly and decisively with individuals who are caught, and 4) publicizing how theft has been dealt with.

If you think theft only happens to the other guy—the unwary entrepreneur who hires the wrong people and then treats them badly—consider the statistics from a recent University of Minnesota survey. Sixty percent of the retail employees who responded to the survey questions admitted they had stolen from their companies in a variety of ways. Typical among dishonest sales clerks was using their discount

112

privileges to make purchases for friends and relatives. Padded expense accounts surfaced among managers and buyers.

Employee theft is by no means limited to retail establishments. Some 30 to 40 percent of the U.S. work force is a bad risk when it comes to handling their companies' merchandise, money, or secrets. Although entrepreneurs would like to trust the employees who work for them, it is unlikely that all of them *can* be trusted.

WHAT ABOUT YOUR LEADERSHIP

If you adopt a practice of not offering feedback, praise, and evaluation you'll be the source of most of your personnel problems. If you start to shortchange your good employees regarding prerequisities, raises, support, etc., it will only be a matter of time before they leave. They might be replaced with employees who are not as good. While it is wise to reduce expenses as much as necessary, not giving your good employees fair compensation and adequate fringe benefits is never recommended. Moreover, in the long run, your operating costs will be much higher if you mistreat your good employees.

FACING THE CHALLENGE

The challenges of personnel problems faced by entrepreneurs aren't for the weak of heart. They require taking a tough stance, talking some turkey and, on occasion, firing people. These problems require taking time out from other day-to-day business operations.

You must strive to handle these problems in a manner that is immediate, professional, and fair. It makes no sense to put your head in the sand and pretend personnel problems don't exist; nor does it make sense to handle one employee one way and another employee a different way. The "easy way" out eventually backfires.

Here are six activities successful entrepreneurs undertake to help diminish personnel problems:

1) Be certain that any organizational policy and procedure guidelines that do exist are understood by your staff.
2) Highlight and make clear from the beginning any specific activities that may be inappropriate to the policies of the company.
3) Seek the help of your peers or associates to gain an added measure of objectivity and impartiality before confronting someone.

113

4) Provide immediate feedback when infractions have been made. Even small transgressions are important, because if they're not dealt with, they often lead to greater problems.

5) Keep a log or chart of inappropriate behavior or activity that can serve as the necessary documentation if the situation grows worse and termination is warranted.

6) Administer a series of response actions—the more frequent or serious the transgression, the greater the penalty leading up to termination.

Recognize that problems will occur, and that employee turnover is a distruptive but common part of the entrepreneurial experience.

CHAPTER 8

Cost and Operation Control

It is the most common and ordinary thing among men to realize, foresee, understand, and predict other men's misfortunes. But, oh, what a rarity it is to realize, foresee, understand, and predict one's own.

—FRANÇOIS RABELAIS

There are hidden costs of going into business—costs that would-be entrepreneurs fail to appreciate until faced with the task of paying them. Let's look at some of these hidden costs in greater detail.

PAYROLL COSTS

Payroll costs are an entrepreneur's bugaboo. Small- to medium-size businesses offer fewer and less comprehensive benefits than large corporations. New entrepreneurs are at a disadvantage when competing for talent. One way to bridge the gap is to offer higher salaries—not a welcome solution—or attempt to sell potential employees on the less frenzied, less stressful environment—a debatable position.

In competing for skilled labor, if you do provide a benefit program, it is likely that the cost of providing such a program to as few as four to eight employees will involve the same level of administrative costs as a program for forty to fifty employees. Thus, cost of benefits per employee in very small businesses can be quite high.

In 1985, entrepreneurs paid an average of $7,000 for employee benefits per full-time salaried employee. The employer's share of FICA-social security payments will see nine rate increases totaling 60 percent between 1970 and 1990. A salary cap of $39,600 annually per employee—the amount on which FICA taxes will be applied—and a FICA rate of 7.65 percent are scheduled for 1990. This means that for any employee earning $39,000 or more, *your* payment for FICA will be over $3,000. Other payroll costs that would-be entrepreneurs often fail to consider include federal and state unemployment insurance, which can average $700 annually per employee.

Next, consider the staggering cost of absenteeism, tardiness, and accrued vacation time. Per full-time salaried employee, that easily averages more than two weeks per year, multiplied by whatever that employee earns per day.

If you introduce a pension benefit insurance program, you'll have to comply with the dozens of ERISA forms listed on page 65.

When it's all added up, employee benefits average almost 30 percent of total compensation and may go higher still. If your business plan includes projected first-year salaries totaling $100,000, you must add at least another $30,000 for benefits. Then, considering Sheldon's Two-Times Law, hold your breath, because the $130,000 figure probably will not be sufficient.

THE HIGH COST OF GOODS SOLD

For each dollar of sales generated in a retail business, what would you guess the cost of goods, that cost of items for resale and other costs directly associated with sale of goods, such as advertising and promotion to be? Based on federal income tax returns ending fiscal year June 1983 for proprietorships operating retail business it was 72.4 percent! For wholesale businesses the average cost of goods sold, which includes all of the expenses described plus sales commissions, was 74.8 percent.

Suppose you want to start a small, incorporated manufacturing concern. The cost of goods sold can average anywhere between 60 and 75 percent of total sales. From the remaining gross profit margin of 25 to 40 percent, all compensation, rents, repairs, fixed expenses of doing business, advertising, interest, taxes, and employee benefits are covered. Perhaps that is why for small incorporated manufacturers, net profits before taxes average only 8.9 percent and in the retail trade business, 2.8 percent.

If your business involves the resale of some type of durable or nondurable good and your sources of supply are concentrated among two or three distributors, you are also in an inherently precarious position. If one of these suppliers can no longer deliver or cannot deliver in the manner and quantity to which you are accustomed and in need, your costs may skyrocket as you turn to alternative, quick-fix solutions. A business that relies on one main source of supply can experience a supply cut-off (or sharp increase in price), find itself with no alternative, and go out of business almost overnight.

It is prudent management to develop multiple sources of supply. Yet because of geography, or your type of business, there may be only one or a few suppliers from which you can efficiently obtain goods for resale.

If your proposed venture is in an industry that operates on a tight gross profit margin (sales minus cost of goods sold equals profit margin), a sudden shrinkage in the gross profit margin can spell disaster. The computations below indicate how a modest increase in fixed costs, coupled with a shrinkage in the gross profit margin, rapidly increases your break-even point.

$$\frac{\$100,000 \text{ Fixed Cost}}{30\% \text{ Gross Profit Margin}} = \$333,333 \text{ Break Even Point}$$

$$\frac{\$104,000 \text{ Fixed Cost}}{27\% \text{ Gross Profit Margin}} = \$385,186 \text{ Break Even Point}$$

$$\frac{\$108,000 \text{ Fixed Cost}}{24\% \text{ Gross Profit Margin}} = \$450,000 \text{ Break Even Point}$$

Are you thinking that the cost of goods sold to you is of no consequence, because you will simply pass this on to the end buyer? Not so. There is an upper limit to what you can charge customers and clients before they will take their business elsewhere. You must remain competitive. Yet because you are small and your buying power is not significant, you are not able to achieve the large volume discounts that larger buyers enjoy. Your costs of goods sold, all other things being equal, will always be higher than those of other larger competitors who can make volume purchase and enjoy discounts.

Higher costs to you would not be such a problem if you were able to offer convenience or some other differentiating service factor. The strategy of offering high customer convenience is practiced by 7-Eleven stores. However, you still could not compete in this market because each 7-Eleven store is part of a comprehensive chain that musters significant buying power.

If you have a healthy cash flow and plenty of warehouse space, you could buy in bulk to take advantage of cash discounts and more favorable terms. You then face increased costs in the form of spoilage and holding costs. You also incur the opportunity cost of having that much money tied up in inventory.

THE HIGH COST OF ENERGY

Despite the perception that the energy crisis is over, smaller businesses pay too much for energy and have few options for change. Small businesses as a collective unit pay marketably higher rates per kilowatt hour of electricity than major industrial users, or even residential users. Though this information is readily available from the U.S. Department of Energy, the small business community keeps biting the bullet without a squawk when it comes to energy costs.

Some argue that the reason the commercial sector—comprised largely of small business—pays more for electricity is that it is more costly for the utilities to provide service to this sector. Not so. Studies commissioned by the Department of Commerce and by the Small Business Administration have demonstrated that the rate of return earned by electric utilities from the commercial sector was greater than that earned from the industrial sector—comprised largely of high-volume users including major corporations.

Various policy and rate-making standards have been introduced over the years. Unfortunately, the typical small business entrepreneur is not in a position to take advantage of declining bloc rates, time of day rates, season and interruptable rates, or any other options suggested.

Small business entrepreneurs seeking to reduce large energy bills have less leeway in adapting energy consumption patterns to off peak hours. Customers, suppliers, and employees may not take kindly to 1:00 A.M. to 5:00 A.M. hours of operation.

Until some startling breakthrough occurs, you are going to light with electricity, heat and cool with natural gas, oil, or electricity; and power equipment by traditional sources—and pay a lot to do it.

MARKETING COSTS PLENTY

Marketing is costly. According to the Cahners Publishing Company, the cost of landing a new account is more than $1,500. This figure represents an average from a study of over 2,400 manufacturers. It includes such items as salaries, commissions, benefits, travel, sales materials, samples, advertising, follow up, and mailings. And the cost of calling on new customers will continue to rise.

Imagine that you have targeted an industrial market and want to market to them by exhibiting at their annual trade show. The cost of exhibiting can range anywhere from $800 to $1,200 in rental fees per eighty square feet of booth space with an additional cost of $3,000 to $4,000 for a professionally designed exhibit. Hopefully, that exhibit can be used again, thus lowering your cost per exhibition. Yet, these are just the entry stakes. Travel to and from the show including air fare, freight or shipping, and accommodations can rival the cost of the booth.

EQUIPMENT PURCHASES, REPLACEMENT, AND UPKEEP

For some strange reason, first-time entrepreneurs whom I've encountered maintain the erroneous notion that to start a business correctly requires purchasing all new equipment. Printers want the newest equipment, engineers want sophisticated Hewlett-Packard calculators, and restaurant owners want sparkling new meat lockers and bread slicers.

There ought to be a law requiring first-time entrepreneurs to buy used equipment, if that equipment is not visible to customers. The customer who comes into your restaurant only cares what the food tastes like, not what the meat locker looks like. Customers who come into your print shop won't even know if the equipment is the latest, even if they see it.

For most businesses, there is no reason to purchase new or the latest version of most equipment. Pick up the magazines in your industry, and flip to the classified section. The "equipment for sale" section is usually substantial. Why? One reason is that so many businesses fail, and there is a lot of equipment being sold at liquidation prices. Another reason is that some of these businesses have been successful, and are ready to buy equipment with greater capabilities. Most of the equipment listed is in good working order and costs 50 percent or less of the "latest."

Particularly when in the business planning stages, it behooves would-be entrepreneurs to obtain the prices of both the latest version of the equipment that they need and of reliable used equipment. In every major city, one can find business equipment brokers who buy, sell, and lease new and used equipment in your industry. It also pays to explore equipment leases. Your first few years will see many changes and the less you have paid up front for heavy artillery, the better positioned you will be to make intelligent changes as growth, revenue, and product patterns emerge.

As has been demonstrated by automobile owners, those who regularly care for their equipment are likely to make it last twice as long or longer. Understandably, the harried and frazzled entrepreneur who already has fifty other things to worry about often doesn't assign equipment maintenance a lofty status. But he ignores equipment maintenance at his peril. To reduce spiraling costs, he shouldn't.

WHAT ELSE DIDN'T YOU COUNT ON?

Will you be buying or leasing a copier? What about the cost of toner and developer? And new paper? You might need a post office box, you will certainly need office cleaning, and you will probably incur your share of overnight express delivery and courier costs.

Are there directories, reference books, and handbooks you will be needing? What about the shelving that goes with them? If you are a proprietorship, some costs that can be expensed as part of a corporation must remain as personal expenditures. For example, there is no provision on the IRS Schedule C for claiming health or disability insurance. The same holds true with dental and medical coverage.

And what about those nitpicking costs charges by the banks and others? They add up! Every time a check is returned or bounced you are looking at $15 to $20. Credit card purchases made on behalf of your business are subject to 14 percent to 18 percent finance charges for payments beyond a specified date. Maintenance and repair of equipment always seem to cost 25 percent to 50 percent more than you planned on.

Inventory pilferage on the part of your employees will break your heart and your wallet. As we saw in the previous chapter, employee shoplifting and pilferage can be crushing. Many companies have introduced attractive product or service discounts to employees as a way of capturing extra sales and reducing the incentive to pilfer. Here again, the discount offered to employees means a reduced gross profit margin and reduced net profitability. However, to the extent that this reduces the pilferage rate, discounts may be desirable.

AVOIDING UNNECESSARY PURCHASES

You'll have to avoid making unnecessary purchases—a prevalent and particularly harmful trap for start-up entrepreneurs. Those in business for themselves quickly realize (1) the speed with which their names get on direct mail lists, (2) the ability of sales reps to find them, and (3) just how deluged with product and service offers an entrepreneur can be.

We have all been influenced by a skillful sales rep who has talked us into buying something that was only marginally needed, not necessary, or frivolous. A few days later, we may find ourselves committed to spending a significant sum for something that we can do without.

If you are incorporated, one solution is to include in your corporate by-laws a clause that states, "All purchase decisions over $X are contingent upon approval by board of directors." This will give you increased leverage for handling unnecessary costs—after all, you are on the board. If your business is a partnership, tell sellers that all purchase decisions are contingent upon approval of the second officer. The officer can be a partner or a department head. If your business is a proprietorship, as a consumer, you have up to three days to rescind any purchase.

LONG-TERM LOCK-INS

In the first few years your business is likely to move. If you have signed a long-term lease and you need to break it, that can generally be arranged. However, in many instances you lose your security deposit, which may be equal to three to six months' rent or more!

I have met countless individuals whose first priority in starting a venture seems to be to plunk down a big wad of cash to secure some "prime" space (much more on locations in Chapter 10). A year or two down the road, and in some cases three to six months, it becomes apparent that they don't need so much space *or* they need more space *or* they need space in a different location.

Business rents, much like any other business expense, tend to increase over time. During your first few years there are far too many variables at play for you to make any long-term location decision. The construction of new facilities is absolutely verboten.

INFLATION WILL BE BACK

As a service to its members and the small business community in general, the National Federation of Independent Business regularly conducts surveys to determine the most pressing issues faced by its members. Since 1979, there's been a strong downward trend in inflation. Understandably, the over 500,000 NFIB members recently indicated that inflation is less of a problem to them—since mid-1980 the number of members who cited inflation as the single most important problem confronting their business was less than 4 percent.

But inflation, similar to energy costs, is a sleeping giant. A change in administration, greater unity among OPEC nations, and international turmoil all can significantly and swiftly fuel the fires of inflation once again.

During the mid- to late 1970s when the United States and much of Western Europe were experiencing record high inflation rates (though these were nowhere near what was experienced in South America and parts of the Middle East), the very nature of business practice was altered. Modest increases in the rate of inflation in the 1990s, and they will come, will place both rookie and veteran entrepreneurs on a spiraling cost juggernaut that may last for years.

SOLUTIONS TO HANDLING COST AND PLUGGING THE REVENUE GAP

There are two basic defenses for handling the spiraling costs that eat into your revenue projections. The first is to *get all the information that you can in advance* on the typical operating costs of businesses in your industry.

A good source is *RMA Annual Statement Studies*, published by Robert Morris Associates, Philadelphia National Bank Building, Philadelphia, PA, 19107. *Annual Statement Studies* can be used as general guidelines but not as in absolute industry norms because the financial statements presented are not selected by any statistically reliable method. However, because *Annual Statement Studies* segments businesses by specific industries and by size of assets, you can generally find data fairly applicable to your own situation.

Another good source of financial information is Dun & Bradstreet's *Cost of Doing Business*. Three separate pamphlets are prepared for proprietorships, partnerships, and corporations. As with *Annual Statement Studies*, there are caveats. The number of firms used in the total sample size is indicated for each line of business. Dun & Bradstreet relies on statistics of income prepared by the statistics division of the Internal Revenue Service. The *Cost of Doing Business* can be obtained by writing the Economic Analysis Department, Dun & Bradstreet Corporation, 299 Park Avenue, New York, NY 10171.

A third source is *The Almanac of Business and Industrial Financial Ratios* by Leo Troy, Ph.D., published by Prentice-Hall, Inc., Englewood Cliffs, NJ 07632. The *Almanac* also relies upon data from the Internal Revenue Service. A key feature is that financial data is presented for twelve different sizes of assets, ranging from under $100,000 to over $250,000,000.

The *Almanac* supplies current performance facts and figures, and aids in answering many cost-related questions such as "Compared to the industry as a whole and to companies of a similar size, how well is my company doing in controlling costs?" Or "What percentage of sales goes to pensions or other benefit plans?" Or "How do my company's outlays on compensation of officers, rents, interest, repairs, and advertising compare with others?"

The second major defense against spiraling costs is to *develop effective internal control procedures.*

Peat Marwick Mitchell & Company points out that not very many years ago a company measured its success by how much of its product it was able to sell. Today entrepreneurs find that success is heavily influenced by the ability to keep costs under control and to maintain a healthy cash flow. Volatile interest rates, shrinking profit margins, and increasing operational costs have caused many entrepreneurs to reassess and upgrade their internal control procedures. It is easier to initiate these procedures in a start-up situation than to change routines once a business is up and going.

Here are traditional control procedures used by successful entrepreneurs for handling payments received, deposits, inventory, supplies, etc. Making sure that all the following are taken care of requires considerable effort. However, if your goal is to keep costs to a minimum, there is no alternative.

Traditional Control Procedures:

Cash, Check Handling

- Is a responsible official assigned to prepare a list of all receipts, both cash and checks, showing from whom amounts were received?
- Is this list made in duplicate on numbered forms, both copies signed by a responsible official and by the cashier?
- Is each day's list of receipts checked against cash book entries?
- Are deposits made daily of each day's receipts intact?
- Are deposits verified with each day's receipts?
- Are all checks received stamped "for deposit only" and deposited within twenty-four hours after receipt?
- Is mail opened by a responsible official other than the bookkeeper or cashier?
- Are all employees who handle cash, merchandise, securities, and other valuables covered by adequate insurance?
- Are each day's receipted deposit slips checked against the day's list of checks and cash received?
- Are bank statements reconciled by someone other than the person authorized to deposit or withdraw funds?
- Are bank statements received and reconciled by someone other than the person in charge of accounting?
- Are cancelled checks examined for evidence of alteration and proper endorsement?
- Are duplicate bank statements requested if errors, erasures, or alterations appear thereon?
- Are the duties of cashier or office assistant and bookkeeper divided between two people?
- Are definite instructions issued that the bookkeeper and cashier may not have access to each other's records?

- Are all checks countersigned by two responsible officials?
- If a check is made out incorrectly, is it voided and a new one issued?
- Are cash disbursement records independently footed and checked against the related general ledger control accounts?
- Are noncash entries covering bad debts, discounts, returns, etc., approved by a responsible official?
- Are accounts reported as uncollectible investigated to determine whether the customer actually exists?
- Are past due accounts periodically reviewed?
- Are accounts receivable test-checked by a person other than the ledger clerk?
- Are payments received electronically verified by someone other than the terminal operator?
- Are employees handling credit memos and adjustments denied access to accounts receivable records?
- Are ledger clerks in credit and collection departments required to switch positions at unannounced intervals?
- Are customers' unpaid balances verified at least once a year by the auditor or a responsible official?
- Are undeliverable verifications investigated?
- Are bookkeepers instructed not to make arbitrary adjustments in customers' ledgers?
- Are all employees required to take annual vacations?
- Are accounting methods and routines recorded in manuals?
- Are all important records physically safeguarded?
- Is an annual audit conducted by a C.P.A. firm?
- Are surprise audits occasionally made?

Payroll

- Are all employees paid by check?
- Is the preparation of payroll and actual payment to employees handled by different employees?
- Is the bank statement for the payroll account reconciled by a responsible official who does not supervise the actual preparation of the payroll?

- Are erasures of dates on time cards carefully checked at frequent intervals?
- Is amount of pay and time worked reviewed independently at irregular intervals?
- Is signing of payroll checks in blank prohibited?
- Are all voided payroll checks retained for review and audit?

Purchasing

- Are purchase invoices attached to checks for payment and the former initialed by check signers?
- Are purchasing and receiving functions separated in order to affix responsibility?
- Are purchases and sales invoices checked to prevent reuse or alterations?
- Are vendors' invoices stamped "Paid" and check numbers and dates of payment noted on invoices?
- Are all returned purchases properly supervised by a responsible employee?
- Are receiving and delivery functions handled by different individuals?
- Are prenumbered vouchers used on merchandise transferred from stockrooms to sales departments?
- Are sales clerks required to initial the vouchers acknowledging receipt of the merchandise?
- Are prenumbered job requisitions used?
- Is the person in charge of the stockroom denied access to the inventory records?
- Is frequent physical inspection of merchandise made by a responsible employee not from the stock departments?
- Is a complete inventory taken at least annually?
- When a physical inventory is made, are employees outside of the department being inventoried used?
- Are the results of the physical inventory compared with the perpetual inventory by a responsible officer?

Shipping

- Are prenumbered shipping tickets used on all deliveries?
- Are both the shipping clerk and the driver required to initial the accounting department's copy of the shipping ticket?

Systems

- Does your billing system interface with other related systems?
- Is billing a centralized function?
- Do you age your receivables on a regular basis?
- Does your order entry system interface with building, inventory, and accounts receivable?

The battle to keep costs under control never ends. Just when you've taken care of one cost area, another slips out of control. You must be ruthless in the allocation of every business dollar. You cannot afford to do less.

CHAPTER 9

Computer System Foul-ups 101

It requires a very unusual mind to undertake the analysis of the obvious.

—ALFRED NORTH WHITEHEAD

The emergence of the computer as a business tool carries with it a whole new set of entrepreneurial pitfalls not experienced by those in previous eras.

You've decided that your business will require, or is ready for, a computer system. Maybe you've found yourself bogged down by clutter and paperwork, or maybe you've felt that a computer is necessary for your new venture. It's true that today's computers, from giant mainframes to comparatively inexpensive personal computers, provide you with the ability to take care of accounting, filing, and typing quickly and easily. Right? Yes, the computer can revolutionize an office, but quickly and easily is the stuff of TV commercials.

BONEHEAD ERRORS?

Ray Kostin, a 46-year-old security services entrepreneur in Tacoma, Washington, was familiar with a couple of software programs he used in his old firm before venturing off on his own. Ray saw real value in computerizing his new venture from the outset. He purchased an IBM-compatible PC, with two disk drives including a 20-megabyte hard disk.

Over a two-week period Ray carefully installed an accounting package, a spreadsheet program, a word-processing program, a database program, and several utilities such as a calendar, a pop-up alarm, a clock, a note pad, and a graphics program. Ray was also careful to copy all these programs individually onto floppy disks that would be held in storage and serve as backups.

One afternoon, Ray was in the middle of a six-hour stint on the computer when he decided to format a couple of *new* floppy disks. Ray had gotten a lot of work done on the computer that day, including the construction of several new files, the preparation of a budget on the spreadsheet program, and several other measures that would improve business operations.

The split second after the formatting program began, Ray realized that he had inadvertently named the wrong disk drive. Instead of formatting the floppy in drive A, Ray ended up formatting the hard disk, which is another way of saying *he erased everything* that was on it.

Ray was crushed. Certainly he could reload all of his programs from backup disks (wisely placed in storage). This was a long, drawn-out process but could effectively be done. The work he had done earlier in the day, including the budget, the accounting records, and so forth, *was gone.* Ray was not in the habit of producing backups on an interim basis. Like most PC users, he preferred to make backups at the end of the day.

Though the work he had done could be duplicated, Ray nevertheless was disheartened. He had saved up his energy and carefully planned his time to be able to spend a long stretch on the computer in the first place. Ray was a fairly proficient computer user and did much of his "composing" as he went along. The thought of having to redo all that work was not palatable. Ray did not keep many notes, and so much of what he had to reconstruct would involve reanalyzing, reestimating, and recalculating almost from scratch.

If you are not familiar with personal computers or with using a hard disk, you might conclude that Ray had made a bonehead error, the likes of which you are not subject to make. However, if you use a computer long enough, the odds are better than even that you will mistakenly erase or damage an important file, unknowingly mistreat your hardware, or otherwise misplace important data. Then there are those who make the mistake of formatting a hard disk. Not many will admit to an error of this magnitude, yet it happens.

Computer equipment is sensitive and requires much greater care than other office equipment. In one celebrated incident, a coffee spill at the *Los Angeles Times* resulted in a computer operations repair bill of $37,000—more than your system will cost, but definitely food for thought.

LET'S GO SHOPPING

In shopping for a computer, you're up against dozens of companies promising state-of-the-art technology, each slightly to very different, with their own benefits and drawbacks. It's easy to stumble into trouble in those woods. What kind of machine is best for your needs? How will your needs change over the years? And will this equipment expand with your business?

As most everyone knows by now the computer, or hardware, itself is only part of the story. Software programs and routines instruct the computer what to do with a certain set of figures, addresses, or calculations. The software available is even more diverse than the hardware, yet the decision is just as important.

What kind of training will be required to administer your system in-house? What about emergency and regular maintenance? What happens if your system suddenly goes blank at 9:00 A.M. Monday morning? Will a technician be on the spot within the hour? Or will you be requested to pack the equipment in its original box and return it to the manufacturer prepaid for servicing?

Many questions need to be asked about the vendor, hardware, software, service, and future expandability before making a purchase. Worst of all, and this is not rare, what happens if you spend a lot of time researching equipment, manufacturers, and suppliers, and buy an expensive computer system, only to find that it is just not appropriate for your business—in other words, only semifunctional. In the face of such a wide choice of technology, these are all common occurrences.

When starting a venture, should you consider installing a computer system if you're not experienced with computers? I say forget the computer for now. Starting a new venture and trying to master a computer is a double whammy.

Learning how to operate a computer and various software programs is so draining on your time that the process will literally conflict with your ability to manage the venture. If you will be assigning staff to the function, fine. But recognize you may fall into the personnel problem discussed in Chapter 7, wherein you are supervising employees who know far more about the equipment and its *use* than you do.

If a computer system does make sense for your situation, let's review what you must ask vendors when considering the purchase or lease of a system.

DEFINE YOUR NEEDS

A reasonable first question to ask yourself is, to the best of your knowledge, how large and complex a system would best support your needs? What business activities do you think should be converted to computer and what are good prospects for future conversion? Make a written list—these are items you will refer to often.

Next, assign priorities to these functions. Some will be much more important than others. What data do you want to input and how would you like it reported back? This affects your software selection. Where would you like it stored, and in what form? This is an important security factor. How many people are going to be performing what functions and how often? Are you in the market for a large mainframe that many employees can share from separate terminals? Or are you looking for a personal computer for yourself, and maybe your secretary, to use occasionally?

You'll have to sit down with your staff, especially the people who will be using the equipment, and discuss their needs. Inform them of what you are considering, and ask for suggestions and comments. Remember, the ones who will be using the equipment will also be the ones who have to put up with its shortcomings.

Prices can range from under $1,000 for a simple PC with a spreadsheet program to tens of thousands of dollars for a mainframe with substations, peripherals, technical support, and emergency backup measures. And it's easy to overlook other costs, such as maintenance, operating costs (including disks and ribbons), training, manuals, and furniture to accommodate the equipment.

Expandability is another important factor in your decision. A

What the Computer Advertisements Promise Versus Reality	
Advertisement	Reality
Reduced paperwork	There is absolutely no evidence of this.
Ease of learning	For all but the most simple program, this is a falsehood.
Versatile	Additional memory and options can be added. However, you may be talked into buying a more expensive system.
A fountain of information at your fingertips	Yes, if the proper input and upkeep is maintained; otherwise, it's garbage-in, garbage-out.
The answer to your problems	An answer, maybe, to one of many problems. Also the introduction of new problems.
Economical	The cost of upgrades and supporting devices virtually unending.

couple of years down the road, you don't want to be stuck with expensive equipment that cannot handle your increased volume, or is not adaptable to changing needs. Conversely, stretching your limited funds for computer equipment, years in advance of future growth, is inefficient use of capital.

CHOOSE THE SOFTWARE FIRST!

Especially when your computer will be serving specialized or essential functions, it is best to choose the software first, and choose the hardware contingent upon that software. Many entrepreneurs are dazzled by the hardware advertisements and think of what runs the system as an afterthought.

There are basically two paths you can follow when choosing software, packaged or customized. If the primary job of your system will be to trace accounts receivable, choosing software that accommodates your industry or business specifically could have great advantage over a standard accounts receivable program chosen on the basis of compatibility with your computer.

132

There are obvious advantages in price with packaged software and in specific applications with custom software. Especially for today's popular PC models, there are literally thousands of programs available with as many different functions. Considering there are millions of personal and small business users of packaged software programs across the country, the programs have become very refined and complete in the past few years. It is quite possible that you will be able to find a packaged software program to fit your needs.

PACKAGED SOFTWARE

To find out which software is best for you, you'll have to rigorously test a few of the types of packages available. Vendor's often offer "demo" disks, short introductions to a particular program. These are excellent places to start, but you have to undertake further research to make an intelligent decision.

Taking an afternoon and performing the same operation on two different types of software offers some indication of what living with your choice will be like. In three hours you may discover a large advantage to one of the programs that would not surface during a ten-minute trial run. Running the program yourself illustrates the ease (or lack thereof) with which it operates.

Do you think your staff could operate this system quickly? Could someone teach them the basics in a few hours? Or will it take a month to lay the groundwork for understanding?

You will have to talk to users of these programs. The best recommendation is from someone who has learned to live with the advantages and disadvantages of a product. Maybe your secretary or clerk has had prior experience with this package. Or maybe you have some friends or acquaintances, preferably in the same business, who use such software. This is not a small decision you are making—there is a great deal of time, money, and effort at stake.

After having checked out the packaged software available you may decide that for your unique applications, packaged software will not do the trick. A popular alternative, cheaper than wholly customized software, is to install a package system and have it customized. Consultants familiar with the type of programs you are interested in can be very helpful with such an installation. With or without a consultant your time investment will be substantial to insure that you achieve your operational goals.

If such conversions cannot be made, there is always customized software. Though generally expensive, in many cases it is necessary. Now, how to go about contracting for this software?

CUSTOMIZED SOFTWARE

As with packaged software, you'll have to decide what your requirements and applications are. This should be drawn up as a proposal request to software vendors. You will need to make it much more complex than a description of what was necessary for packaged software. Because vendors will be catering to your specific needs, any omission, overestimate, or underestimate on your part will be costly. But then again, an advantage of custom software is that it is possible to alter the program or programs more precisely to your purposes.

One possibility is to seek both the hardware and the software from the same vendor; this would eliminate the chance of problems between separate systems. Your concerns must be posed to each potential vendor in the early stages of the transaction—later it may be too late.

In your software and/or computer system proposal you will have to include a very detailed discussion of your needs and applications. You should include the following:

- an overall discussion of your business activity
- specific activities you will want to computerize
- the number, size, and capacity of equipment you seek (e.g., the number of terminals and their location, the amount of data storage you will need)
- who will be using the equipment and how
- what kind of goals you expect from equipment use

Distribute your proposal requests to several companies, at least three, to insure that you will have enough responses for a meaningful comparison. Too many proposals will bog you down and delay your decision.

EXAMINING VENDORS

There are many important factors you'll have to consider when examining potential vendors, such as the vendor's track record, financial status, and management. You will need to be certain that you can reach

134

this company when you have a question or problem—response times to your calls for service and support may be critical. How long have they been in this type of business? And what if they go out of business? If you do not know the answer to these questions, start searching. Research their financial strength. The Chamber of Commerce, Dun & Bradstreet, or the Better Business Bureau are good places to start. Get their balance sheets or annual reports if possible.

What about the vendor's experience with your type of needs? How many other customers with similar needs do they have? Get client references. Do you know the size of the firm, the number of employees, and the qualifications of the branch manager? Such information will be helpful when making your choice.

You need to make a decision based on the permanence of vendors. You may have some serious headaches if they change to other product lines. A computer-related problem that no one knows how to resolve adequately could have drastic effects on your ability to continue using that system, and on your ability to stay in business.

EXAMINING VENDOR'S PROPOSALS

In assessing each proposal you must complete the initial review of each vendor. Eliminate any vendors about whom you have serious doubts immediately, no matter how good their proposals may sound. Arrange to meet another time with those vendors who seem qualified and get a second demonstration of their products. Be wary of any who do not provide adequate demonstrations, or any who cannot adequately answer your questions.

Here are factors you must consider for each vendor's computer system or software proposal:

- Equipment configuration—Are the proposed number of units enough? Do its operating characteristics and space needs fit your location? Is it expandable to meet any future needs you have outlined?

- Financial considerations—Are you renting or buying the equipment? Are you seeking economy? Is service and technical support included and for what length of time?

- Service and technical support—Besides the cost of this support, how comprehensive is it and what specifically are you offered? Will a trained engineer be available to assist immediately in case

135

of a problem? What about personnel training and back-up support?

Make a chart of the benefits and disadvantages of each proposal and ask the people who will be using the equipment to comment on each.

Once you have narrowed down your choices considerably, it is essential that you check references. No one will be able to give you a better idea of how well a vendor performed than a reference. The vendor will probably be able to provide a list of selected references, but dig further, to find those installations where all may not be well. You will need at least to ask the reference such general questions as: How efficiently (on time? on budget? installed properly?) did the vendor install the system? Did the system work as effectively as you had hoped? Were you satisfied with the vendor's performance? Would you use this vendor again yourself? And would you recommend this vendor to others?

Specifically, you will want to ask questions about the type of software system installed, whether or not it is standard or customized, and did it measure up to the vendor's claim?

You must be ready to compare the various contracts in detail and solicit the input of those who have worked with the vendors and/or the systems. Items to check on vendor contracts include: guarantees, warranties, and back-up services, participation in systems analysis, and provisions for installation, training, and support. Are you sure you covered all the criteria of your original plans? Go back over your original notes and double-check. Do your employees seem to be content with your choice? By now, you should have picked up enough information to make a responsible decision about a computer system.

Most vendors will have some form of standard contract, yet you must not let this limit your control. If there is something you feel should be in the contract, especially if it is an item concerning your security, make all efforts to include it. The language and requirements you use in the contract must be very specific, as with all contracts. It is always a good idea to have your lawyer go over it before the final approval to insure that there are no snags. Also, negotiate. Negotiate the price, date of completion, or anything else you feel can be improved (or maybe you would just prefer it improved).

Nothing is final in a contract until it is signed by both parties. Too many entrepreneurs create artificial urgency in their minds. Avoid rushing just to complete the deal. You'll be better off to take a little extra time. Attempting to make changes after the contract is signed may be like barking at the moon.

THE ACID TEST

Once the contract has been signed, sealed, and delivered, and the equipment has been installed, you still will not be able to relax. The fun has only begun. Even if you are confident that you have purchased the best computer equipment and software money can buy, including impeccable service, support, and clear operating instructions, it hardly means that things will go smoothly from here on.

The most appropriate and advanced equipment will accomplish nothing if your staff doesn't understand how to use it. Entrepreneurial headaches multiply in direct proportion to the amount of equipment you've acquired.

It may take a while for everything to work out for the best. You'll need to keep plenty of attention focused on the system and the people who are using it. During the weeks and months following installation you'll have to keep a sharp eye on the following:

- Make sure everything is in working order
- Oversee the training of the employees
- Test the programs to insure compatibility with desired results—this is especially important with custom software—because certain characteristics of the software will probably not show up before heavy use
- Convert old format files and information onto the new system—this would be a good time to clear out any ancient or unnecessary files
- Double-check to make sure all runs smoothly
- Develop methods for analyzing system effectiveness

With careful supervision, you'll be one of the lucky ones who is able to acquire a cost-efficient system that serves your needs with a minimum of headaches.

CHAPTER 10

A Matter of Location

Nothing endures but change.

—HERACLITUS

Choosing an appropriate business location is one of the most difficult tasks facing entrepreneurs in retailing, wholesaling, manufacturing, or business services. For professional service firms, the question of location is of lesser importance because of the relative mobility and ease with which professional service firms may relocate. It has been said that the three most important factors when considering residential real estate are location, location, and location. The same holds true for retail operations and business services. Let's examine entrepreneurical pitfalls in this area first.

Before choosing a retail or business services location (note: business services include shoe, watch, and appliance repair; barber shops and beauty salons; laundry, mailbox, and storage services; and equipment, video, and other rental shops), it is necessary to define your business in the broadest terms and determine long-term objectives. These tasks should be undertaken when preparing the business plan.

Many entrepreneurs erroneously believe that it is sufficient to obtain information on the demographics of the population in the trade area, i.e., age, income, and size of family; competition; and traffic data. These factors are important, and all retail and business services locational analysis should properly include them. But once a tentative location has been identified, and given that the traditional demographic analysis reveals many positive factors, there are still a host of other factors that must be checked before a final commitment is made.

RETAIL COMPATIBILITY

Tom Hargrave opened his small restaurant on the far left end of a neighborhood shopping center off Route 18—one of the major roads in town that included a center meridian. Since Tom's business was the last one on his side of the strip, (see diagram below) Tom had no neighbors to his left. To his right, in order, were a pet shop, a hardware store, a convenience goods store, a post office branch, and an appliance repair shop.

Located directly across from Tom was a barber shop, a quick print shop, a toy store, a medical aids and devices retail outlet, and a Radio Shack store. Tom's research revealed that hundreds of vehicles entered the common parking lot each day. The shopping area itself had adequate name recognition among consumers in the trade radius. Most of the other merchants were doing well, many having been in the present location for three years or more.

Tom felt certain that with the amount of traffic the shopping center was already pulling in, with some good advertising, good word of mouth, first-rate decor, and great food, it would only be a matter of time before he would be doing a bustling business. Tom had considered a location up the road in the regional mall, but the lease was nearly three times as costly, and he feared getting lost among the surrounding competing restaurants.

In the weeks that followed the grand opening, Tom quickly observed that business was pretty good from 11:00 A.M. to 2:30 P.M., fair from 2:30 to 5:00 P.M., and threadbare after 5:00 P.M. Though his menu

Neighborhood Shopping Center

Tom's Restaurant		Barber Shop
Pet Shop		Quick Print
Hardware		Toy Store
7-Eleven Store		Medical Aids
Post Office		Radio Shack
Appliance Repair		

(Meridian)

— ROUTE 18 —

included some special dishes that Tom felt were sure to please, very few customers were ordering them.

Originally, Tom had not wanted to do any take-out business. He felt that this would conflict with his intended image. However, it became apparent to Tom that unless he offered take-out, revenues would suffer greatly. Tom also rolled back the prices on his menu and eliminated some of the higher-cost specialty dishes.

His clientele, which consisted largely of the regular patrons of surrounding stores, were impulse diners. They stopped in Tom's restaurant because they were in between errands and needed a break, in a hurry and just wanted to pick up something for the road, or worked in the area and found it to be convenient.

Though Tom had spent a bundle on fixtures and decor, he began to realize that as a small restaurant in a convenience goods neighborhood shopping area, "fancy" was not needed, and certainly was not sought by patrons.

One Saturday, while Tom was attending a seminar on marketing, he learned that business compatibility is a key factor in the collective draw of retail businesses in the immediate area. Tom learned that being located next to a pet store and an appliance repair shop, for example, actually had negative impact on his business.

While he had settled in comfortably and was doing moderately well, to achieve his original goals, Tom would need to be located in a shoppers' goods location. Had Tom elected to be located next to a movie theater, other restaurants, men's and women's clothing stores, home furnishing stores, and office buildings, his plan for building a quality restaurant might have been possible.

CONVENIENCE vs. SHOPPERS' GOODS

Will you be located next to businesses that will generate store traffic for your business? For example, if you were offering shoppers' goods items, such as men's and women's clothing, major appliances, or expensive jewelry, it is best to locate near other stores carrying shoppers' goods. Conversely, as Tom discovered, if you are located in a "convenience goods shopping area," including such stores as a supermarket, a hardware store, a bakery, a package store, or drugstore, the best way to take advantage of business compatibility would be to also open a convenience goods store.

Take a look at the shopping centers in your own area and invariably you will find a clothing store or shoe store located in an otherwise all convenience goods shopping area. It is my bet that the number of days these stores have in that location are limited. They simply will not generate the traffic, vehicular or pedestrian, necessary to be successful in that location.

With the advent of super malls and regional shopping centers, often shoppers' goods and convenience goods outlets will be found coexisting under the same roof. In this situation it is important to be located in a section of the shopping complex that is conducive to what you are offering. For example, a gift shop is generally well located if it is next to a general merchandise or department store, a theater, an eating place, or anywhere where lines of patrons form (and thus have several minutes to observe the front window display). A pet store should not be located immediately adjacent to a restaurant, dress shop, or salon— it will not help either merchant.

How important is retail compatibility? For a small retail store in its first year of operation, with limited funds for advertising and promotion, retail compatibility can be the single most important factor in survival.

MERCHANT ASSOCIATIONS

Most first-time business owners have no idea how effective and crucial a strong merchants' association can be in promoting and maintaining the business in a given area. When considering any retail location, the presence (or lack thereof) of an effective merchants' association is a vital factor.

What if there is no merchants' association? Generally, but not always, a shopping center with no merchants' association (or an ineffective one) is often on the decline. This is characterized by excessive litter or debris in the area, vacant stores, or a parking lot in need of repair. It is best to avoid any locations with these symptoms, and with a little investigation they can be avoided. Still, I'm amazed at the number of new businesses that are started in third-class shopping strips, or visibly ratty locations. The desire of some to start a business transcends common sense.

A good merchants' association can strengthen your business and save you money through group advertising programs and group insurance and security measures. Some associations have literally induced city planners to add highway exits near their shopping centers! Other associations have lobbied for and received funds from the city to remodel or renovate their shopping centers, including extension of parking lots, refacing of buildings, or installation of better lighting. Additionally, merchants' associations can be particularly effective in promotion of the stores based on a common theme, holiday, or event. The collective draw can be several times that of a single merchant.

How can you determine if the retail location you're considering could benefit from an effective merchants' association? Ask other store owners in the area who the officers of the association are, how often the group meets, what the yearly dues are, and what specifically has been accomplished in the last twelve months. Also ask to see a copy of the last meeting minutes. Determine what percentage of the members were in attendance.

RESPONSIVENESS OF THE LANDLORD

Directly related to the appearance of a retail location is the responsiveness of the landlord to the individual merchant's needs. Unfortunately, many landlords hinder the operation of the business and are responsible for the demise of their own properties.

In countless instances, landlords have thwarted business owner's attempts to generate more business by restricting the placement and size of signs, by foregoing (or ignoring) needed repairs and maintenance, or by renting adjacent retail space. Some indiscriminately rent to businesses that are not compatible, or that are in direct competition with present tenants. Often landlords lack the funds to maintain their properties, and rather than continuing to invest in their holdings by maintaining a proper appearance and supporting the tenants, they instead try to squeeze the property for whatever they can get.

To determine if the landlord is responsive, you must talk to the tenants before moving in yourself. Does the landlord return calls promptly, and are service people dispatched in a timely manner? Or is the landlord simply collecting the rent and then disappearing? Does the landlord have any policies that hamper marketing innovations? Many do.

You should also contact the previous tenants of the location you have in mind. This will provide invaluable information. Find out what business they were in and why they left. Did they fail, or move to larger quarters? What support or hindrances did the landlord provide? If the opportunity presented itself, would they be the retail tenants of the landlord again?

ZONING AND PLANNING

Your town's zoning commission will be happy to provide you with the latest mapping of the retail location and surrounding area that you're considering. Find out if there are restrictions that will limit or hamper your operations. Will construction or changes in city traffic routing serve as barriers to your store? Will any locational advantages you may presently have be diminished by changes in zoning? Most zoning boards, along with economic/regional development committees, do several years' advance planning and can provide valuable insights for an entrepreneur considering locations.

Relating to zoning, what is your intended length of stay and your lease agreement? Do you plan to operate the business in your first location indefinitely, or have you determined a set number of years? If the business is successful, will you be able to expand at the initial location? Then is your lease flexible so that you have an option to renew after a specified number of years? The time to consider these factors is before you settle on a location!

LEASE CONSIDERATIONS

As if you didn't have enough, here are items you'll have to consider in seeking a lease for commercial space according to Robert S. Cunningham, vice president of the Real Estate Brokerage Subsidiary of Spaulding and Slye of Boston, MA.

1. How long will the lease run? Typically, commercial leases run from three to ten years. These terms are too long for start-up entrepreneurs. (Hopefully, subleasing, number 4 below, is available.) The lease should spell out what happens if the space isn't ready by the moving date. Allow an extra three weeks beyond the date the landlord says the space will be ready.

2. How much is the rent and how is it determined? Although commercial rents are generally measured by the annual cost per square foot of space, there may be numerous variations that greatly affect your monthly payment. Also, how many months'

security deposit is required? For start-up firms, you may have to offer a sum equal to six months' rent or more!

3. Are there escalator clauses? If you'll be the first tenant in a space, the landlord will not have precise information as to the cost of providing this space (i.e., utilities). Therefore, you must be on guard against escalator clauses that are tied to indices that do not reflect the true costs of operation.

4. Are there subleasing opportunities? One or two years after signing a long-term lease you may realize that much more space is necessary. If you have the option to sublease, many problems can be averted. New tenants will have to meet the same standards that the owner applies to other tenants, and if the new tenant pays more than you did for the rent, an agreement will have to be reached on who keeps the profits.

5. Renewal capabilities. Once the present lease expires, the landlord has no legal obligation to offer the same space to you. Thus it is important that a renewal option be included in your lease agreement that guarantees you'll have first rights to the space at the prevailing market rate when your lease expires.

6. What if the landlord goes broke? To avoid against this possibility, your lease should contain a standard "recognition" or nondisturbance clause.

7. What about insurance? Find out if there is a comprehensive insurance policy for all tenants and exactly what the policy entails. Frequently, a landlord with many tenants has a hodgepodge of overlapping and inadequate coverage. In general, landlords are expected to carry a comprehensive policy on the building that covers liability for common areas and provides casualty protection for the building itself. Landlords usually have the right to insist that tenants carry their own insurance to protect the landlord against claims that might arise from the conduct of individual businesses. You must be sure that the policies dovetail, so you should get a professional insurance agent or a lawyer with a background in insurance.

8. Are all building services spelled out? You must obtain precisely what services you're entitled to in writing as part of your lease. These might include:

    electricity
    heating, ventilation, and air-conditioning

145

> cleaning
> security

9. Who pays for improvements? This provision is usually open to negotiation and the best negotiator gets the best deal. Landlords are more prone to pay the bills for major renovation work if the items requested will attract future tenants after you move.

    Agreements about renovations must be put in writing and be accompanied by a detailed floor plan with an estimate of costs from a contractor before the lease is signed. This document is called the work letter and should specify who *owns* any improvements. Unless agreed otherwise, the landlord can claim ownership of all improvements.

OVERCOMING A TOUGH RENTAL AGENT

Sometimes you'll have to fight for the space you want. Others may be seeking it, or the leasing agent may dislike your type of business. The following are strategies that entrepreneurs have used for overcoming or neutralizing the effects of a difficult rental or property manager:

- Business gift—this could involve tickets to the theater, gift certificate to an expensive restaurant, set of Cross pens and pencils, or bottle or case of expensive liquor.

- Discussion with other tenants—talk to other tenants, particularly those near your location, to determine if the rental agent is difficult with everyone or just you; what his "hot buttons" are (what makes him happy); and the best way to deal with him in the future.

- Obtain the developer's annual report—from this report, you can obtain the names of higher-ups within the company, some of whom you may already know. If none of the individuals is familiar to you, attempt to find out what organizations they belong to, then try to meet them socially or work out a meeting through a mutual friend.

- Slug it out—by slugging it out, I mean call the agent every day and send mail and messengers that urge him to capitulate. Also, arrange meetings with him as often as possible.

- Over his head—under this strategy you simply determine who his boss is and who his boss's boss is and attempt to deal with them and not him.

OTHER CONSIDERATIONS

Here is a quick review of considerations when choosing a retail or business services location.

- How much retail, office, and storeroom space is needed?
- Is parking space available and adequate?
- Can special lighting, heating or cooling, or installations be installed if necessary?
- Will external lighting in the area attract evening shoppers?
- Will increased advertising expenses be needed if a more remote location is selected?
- Is public transportation available?
- Can the area serve as a source of supply of employees?
- Is there adequate fire and police protection?
- Will sanitation or utility service be a problem?
- Are customer restroom facilities available?
- Is the perceived accessibility to the store adequate?
- Are external awnings or decks present to provide shelter during inclement weather?
- Will crime insurance premiums be excessive?
- Is it convenient for pick up and/or delivery?
- Is the trade area heavily dependent upon seasonal business?
- Is the location convenient to your residence?

PROCEED WITH CAUTION

Choosing a location is, at best, a risky undertaking. Considering the consequences of choosing a location that proves to be unsuitable, it pays to get as much assistance as possible. (Where have you heard that before?) The local chamber of commerce in a city of at least 100,000 people will usually have a division devoted primarily to assisting entrepreneurs in finding locations. This a free service that surprisingly few people take advantage of. The Small Business Administration's 108 offices throughout the U.S. can provide help.

You may need to hire a consultant to analyze two or three locations that you have selected. If this is the case, it is far more cost effective to provide the consultant with preselected potential locations, rather than initiate open-ended searches.

Other sources of information on potential locations include bankers and lawyers who are familiar with locations where their clients were previously located. Realtors can also provide information on locations, but they may be biased since their compensation is based upon commissions for renting property.

Selection of a retail or business services location requires time. It should *not* be done hastily to concur with a loan approval. If a suitable location has not been found, postpone your plans and do not plan to open until a suitable location is secured. A few months' delay is only a minor setback compared to massive problems that result from a poor location.

MANUFACTURING AND WHOLESALING LOCATIONS

There are scores of considerations in evaluating a retail or business services location. However, such a task is in no way near the complexity of evaluating a location for a manufacturing firm or a wholesaling and distributing operation. You must get help from the beginning.

Undoubtedly, you will encounter real estate brokers and/or developers who may offer various package deals. A professional real estate broker must have your best interests in mind when recommending a plant location. He/she must not be following hidden agendas, i.e., trying to sell you on properties that he/she represents exclusively or for which he/she will receive additional consideration or favors from others.

There are consultants who specialize in industrial locations. For a fee they can guide you through the entire planning phase. Many leading banks, major utilities, and in some areas, local governments provide such specialists for no fee. These professionals, who generally remain unbiased in their assessment of various locations, are literally invaluable.

With the emergence of organized industrial parks, many of the start-up headaches for new manufacturing or distributing operations are diminished. Still, it is important to carefully review the terms of leases and determine to what degree lease convenants are enforced. You have probably figured out that choosing a location also requires the services of an attorney, perhaps an engineer, more than likely a contractor or two, a banker, an insurance agent, and a good accountant.

It is not unusual to be evaluating locations for a year or more. This may seem like an inordinate wait before starting a business, yet the costs of choosing a poor location can be far greater than the cost of delaying an opening.

As with any major commitment to a business location, all conditions and terms must be in writing. If it is not in writing, it doesn't exist.

SOME SIMILAR ANALYSES

Many of the steps used to evaluate a specific site are similar to those that should be undertaken for a retail location analysis. For example, check with nearby businesses to determine what problems, if any, exist and how they may be avoided. If your plans call for leasing a turnkey operation, it is important to check the reputation and experience of the architect and the builder. No building, plant, or location is perfect and once you have settled in one, this fact will become abundantly clear.

Business compatibility is particularly important for manufacturers. Will you be locating next to other companies that operate somewhat similarly to you? If so, you may benefit from existing transportation facilities and supply lines that may result in lower overall costs than could be achieved otherwise. Here is a checklist of additional items:

- Is there adequate police and fire protection in your area? In unincorporated areas, this may not be a given. In such circumstances, you may incur higher insurance costs and/or the expense of a security service.
- Is mail delivery and telephone service in this area adequate?
- Does this site include a showroom that is readily accessible to buyers and customers?
- Will you be located near support services such as banks, the post office, hospitals, libraries, and shopping facilities?
- What is the availability of utilities, including electricity and gas? Also what about the availability of natural gas and alternative fuel sources for heating and processing?
- What is the adequacy of the water supply, the water pressure, and its quality?
- Are there sewers, and what is their elevation?
- How is waste disposal handled?

149

THE LABOR FORCE

Depending on the size of your operation, the characteristics of the surrounding labor force may need to be examined further. Is there an abundance of skilled labor in your area that will support operations? Or are unskilled laborers, undesirable union practices, and other factors at play that may jeopardize an efficient operation? How accessible is your location to potential employees? Is public transportation available? What is the wage structure in the area? Often wage rates in a locale are greatly influenced by a large corporation. The workers you thought you could hire at so much per hour may have expectations of several dollars more.

MORE QUESTIONS

Inside the plant or buildings, are the shipping and loading areas adequate? Are safety devices in place such that you can get past the stringent requirements of the Occupational Safety and Health Administration (OSHA)? What escape routes are there in the event of fire or other major hazards? Are special foundations needed for heavy equipment? If so, you may find yourself shelling out funds to reinforce or replace portions of a plant floor. What condition is the central heating and air-conditioning unit in and is it adequately located?

You also will have to check local zoning ordinances. How restrictive are the zoning ordinances? Are there restrictions that will specifically hamper your activities? What are the regulations in regards to parking and employee-to-parking-space ratios?

Will your business be violating pollution control standards and prompt a tax by the EPA and other local environmental agencies? Remember pollution also includes noise as well as air and water. In terms of community relations, will your business have at least adequate "curb appeal"—this can be useful in community standing as well as appealing to visiting clients and customers.

Also, is parking allowed on the street, and what are the overnight and weekend restrictions? Are the streets surrounding your plant publicly or privately operated and maintained? Will you be responsible for sweeping, repair, maintenance, snow removal, and repaving of the roadway?

ENTREPRENEURIAL LOCATION FEVER

Far too many entrepreneurs go about choosing a business location with too short a time perspective. Remember Sheldon's Three Times Law. What generally happens when somebody starts out to choose a business location is that they start clipping ads out of the paper, visit a few sites, talk to some people, draw up a list of parameters, and still don't know what to do.

For retail and business services locations, some entrepreneurs fall in love with a site and collect evidence that supports their instantaneous decision, believing that they have undertaken a proper analysis. The personal preferences of the entrepreneur are part and parcel of any site selection, but when a site is selected for emotional reasons (the entrepreneur enjoys the status of a certain location) or for reasons of personal convenience (the location is minutes from the entrepreneur's residence), the business may suffer.

Much can go wrong in the selection of manufacturing and wholesaling operation locations and it usually does. Since location selection in this case contains so many variables and can be so overwhelming, there is a strong tendency among entrepreneurs to "get it over with," "make do," and "take care of it later." Rather than continue to assess additional locations to find one that is closer to the ideal, anxious, bedazzled, action-oriented types (read "entrepreneur") tend to suboptimize. They choose a location that is good, as opposed to continuing to look a bit longer for one that is excellent.

PROFESSIONAL SERVICE FIRM LOCATIONS

The pitfalls inherent in the selection of a professional service firm location are far less treacherous than those for retail and business services, and manufacturing and wholesaling operations. The primary reason is that a service firm derives its revenue by the delivery of a nontangible good, mainly the service. Thus such items as raw materials, inventories, shelving, loading docks, and the like are minimized or virtually unnecessary.

Still, the office location of an attorney, doctor, or dentist, a realtor and so on, is important. It can convey an image of prosperity to prospective clients and patients. Some of the considerations discussed above apply to professional service locations particularly in the areas of parking, security, accessibility, compatibility, and responsiveness of the landlord or leasing agent.

Let's examine the key components of office atmospherics—the message your professional service location conveys to others. In what shape is the exterior appearance of the building? Is there an outdoor sign or directory in the lobby? Is parking available? Are you located in an appropriate district?

If the building has a lobby, what is the decor? Does it need to be modernized? Is the lobby clean and well lit? Approaching your office, what is the appearance of your door and the sign or lettering? When visitors first enter, do they notice shabby, worn carpeting and marks on the wall? Or is your reception area spiffy, well maintained, and contemporary? Is the layout cramped? Or are there clear open passageways to enter the office? Is the reception area located in an area where other offices are screened from initial view? This is important to convey a quality image.

In what condition are the office hallways? Are they clean, well lit, and covered with new rugs? Is the overall decor pleasing? The appearance of your office and its surroundings may well influence the fees you are able to charge, and hence your profitability.

CHAPTER 11

Passing the Collection Plate

The use of money is all the advantage there is in having it.

—BENJAMIN FRANKLIN

Have you noticed how many doctors and dentists have adopted a policy of asking you to pay *right now*, on your way out the door? Have you considered how many new opportunities there are to use your major credit card at places that aren't even oriented toward retail sales, from the pledge you make during a public television fund-raiser to the refreshments you order to help a local service organization?

There is a good reason for immediate payment and credit card use. The experience of most businesses is that collecting payment is difficult and time consuming, and best avoided or left up to the credit companies that specialize in such activity. In fact, collecting debts is a large enough problem to merit its own industry. Consider collection

153

departments of sizable stores and companies, independent collection agencies, and accountants and lawyers who specialize in collection problems and litigation.

Many entrepreneurs will be caught up in the collections dilemma at some point. Some will be so mired in collection problems that the doors of the business will close for good.

WITH SUCCESS COMES COLLECTIONS

Two women started a public relations firm in Utah called GJ Communications. This was the first public relations firm in their small but growing city. They marketed their services by word of mouth only, since it was a particularly effective method, and kept marketing costs at a minimum. One of their early clients traded them office space for some retainer services.

With little capital investment, they were able to fill a service vacuum with no competition. Things were rosy indeed. GJ Communications soon grew to four full-time staffers, several part-time employees, and a healthy roster of free-lancers who could be called upon as needed.

The client list grew. In addition to numerous local clients—from the retailers' association at the one shopping mall in town to the one theatre in town—the firm managed to attract business from some national companies based in nearby Salt Lake City.

Traditionally, public relations is not a service area where one asks for payment up front or as a client is walking out the door. Rather, contracts are signed that include payment schedules, usually as major segments of projects are completed.

GJ Communications dutifully sent invoices as these segments were completed, causing the partner in charge of the bookkeeping to comment: "Just keeping track of invoices and sending them out on time was enough of a headache, especially since we were at a volume that was just too small to justify computerizing. When customers didn't pay and had to be reinvoiced and phoned, things got really crazy. I didn't want, and couldn't afford, to work full-time chasing down bad accounts, but that's what was happening."

Two years into the business, the region's economy went into a tailspin. As money became tight, debtors became very slow to pay. Some clients filed for bankruptcy and never paid GJ (or any other creditors). Others paid their other creditors first, knowing that GJ would never spend the money or time to really go after them. Debtors chose to pay suppliers, lawyers, and banks well ahead of payments to a public relations firm.

"The cash flow problem was our downfall," explained a GJ partner about the firm's decision to close its doors after three years. "Oddly enough, we had plenty of clients. We just didn't have much in the way of reliable business that would pay our bills in a reasonable amount of time. About 15 percent of our clients paid promptly and about 25 percent paid after a second or third invoice. But 60 percent either never paid or paid only after we'd spent so much time invoicing and calling that it was barely worth it."

The slower paying a charge account becomes the more difficult it is to collect.

Collection Difficulties Over Time	
Time Overdue	Proportion Collectible
Over sixty days	89%
Over six months	67%
Over twelve months	45%
Over twenty-four months	23%
Over thirty-six months	15%
Over five years	Forget it!

Retail businesses that seem like "cash on the barrelhead" types, from restaurants to dry cleaners, are not immune to similar collection problems like those suffered by professional service businesses. Hundreds of hours can be eaten up trying to collect on bad checks or personal lines of credit.

IT'S MORE THAN TIME AND MONEY

As if time and lost revenue collection difficulties aren't bad enough, additional problems occur when payments are consistently late or altogether uncollectible. Several of these are discussed below.

Added interest expense

When you are not able to collect on accounts due, you may need to borrow, or borrow more than originally anticipated, to maintain business as usual, which incurs added interest expense. Also these borrowed funds were probably not factored into your early estimates of the capital needed to get and stay in business.

Debts

When cash flow slows to a trickle because of collection difficulties, one unhappy answer is to slow down payments to your own suppliers and creditors. This means mounting debts. Disgruntled creditors will write and phone you and levy late charges. Some may even cut off your credit. Yet, you need them.

Tied up capital

Even if you have the capital to keep out of debt, and can avoid borrowing when collection problems arise, supporting slow collections is always a poor use of business capital. How much more profitable it would be if you could put that capital to work in a way that enhances the business rather than simply keeps it alive.

Bookkeeping problems

The more you have to invoice, reinvoice, and wait for payments, the more complex your bookkeeping becomes. Revenues and expenses don't readily balance, and projections for the future are difficult. You may even have to hire additional bookkeeping help, another unanticipated expense.

Borrowing difficulties

When your accounts show a substantial amount in "collectibles," with little real knowledge of when, or whether, collections can be made, potential lenders become skeptical. That loan application you had counted on for expansion or equipment may suddenly be rejected.

Competition

All of these difficulties offer a good opening for the competition, new or old, in your market. Suddenly your business, which began with so much real promise, seems stuck in its tracks. You find yourself with little capital left for marketing or growing to capture the competitive edge.

WHO GETS CREDIT?

Many collection difficulties could be avoided if there were a way to give credit only to the most credit worthy and demand cash from others. Unfortunately, this just isn't feasible for many new businesses. Typically, a new business is happy to get clients and customers of any kind and is not in a position to risk losing them by demanding cash until they prove themselves worthy of credit. Additionally, asking for cash payments just isn't the way business is done in many circumstances. Large contracts or lengthy projects receive payment upon completion, or at least upon completion of specific segments.

Imagine how you would feel if you hired a new construction firm to build an addition to your house and they wanted payment up front. First, you might wonder about the firm's ability to deliver if it couldn't begin work before payment. Second, you might wonder how you could protect yourself against unsatisfactory work if you had already made payment. New firms need to establish good will, and often that means risking collection difficulties.

A TOUGH PROBLEM FOR CONTRACTORS

When James Tate, a Florida contractor, started his own construction firm, he began by taking on contracts with no progress payments. He had assembled a crew of laborers and craftsmen whom he needed to keep busy, and obtaining construction contracts the fastest and easiest way—on a signature and a promise—seemed to be the solution.

"I went through my start-up capital within a few months, just paying my men and buying materials," he reported. He managed to delay some construction starts until clients made initial payments that would allow him to purchase materials. "I reasoned that at least I wouldn't be out-of-pocket with the lumber and concrete companies," he notes.

When collections, which could average six to eight months, still presented problems, Tate began a policy of working only for customers he knew or who came highly recommended. However, that didn't hasten overall collections either.

"It's unbelievable, but you can't even count on friends and associates to come through with their payments. You can bump into them at a party or in the street, and they don't even bat an eye about the fact that they owe you thousands of dollars. What's worse is that you feel like such a dog for badgering friends for money they owe you."

Now before construction begins, Tate factors in materials, wages, and some profit when seeking partial payment. And he alerts clients that payments will be due at specific points along the way. "And I still have problems collecting," he says.

"Sure, I could stop construction, but that would be cutting off my nose to spite my face. I'm in business to build, and I need to keep the men building if I ever hope to make a go of it. I think the only people that can really afford this slow payment problem are those that have so much money to begin with that they really don't need to be running a business at all!"

Tate may be exaggerating the costs of getting into business, but he is not overestimating the frustration of collections and the need to anticipate collection problems as a real cost of doing business. For new businesses, failure to realistically calculate these costs can be as serious as underestimating the cost of start-up inventory, taxes, and payroll.

CREDIT CHECKS

Credit checks are one way that many businesses approach the question of who gets credit, but these present their own problems. First, credit checks require a substantial investment in time and energy. Second, they require expertise in interpreting the meaning of the facts you uncover about someone's seeming ability to pay.

A good report from a credit bureau or bank simply means that the individual or firm in question generally pays. It doesn't mean that payment comes as quickly as you would like. And, of course, there are no guarantees. Many firms maintain good credit ratings down to the last day before bankruptcy, which may be the day your invoice arrives on their desks.

If you do decide to check on credit, you'll need to educate yourself on what to ask. Your bank may be able to get information from a potential customer's bank, or you may have to get it yourself. The answers to any of the following questions will be helpful:

- How long has the customer had an account?
- What is the average balance of the account?
- What is the customer's credit rating with the bank?
- Does the customer have a loan?

- Is the loan secured? What kind of security?
- When is the loan due?

You can't be certain of getting all the answers. Often, you'll get general ballpark figures rather than specifics. Further complicating the situation, many firms or individuals whose credit you might check do not keep all their financial matters within one, or even two, institutions. They may have several different accounts and loans with different banks.

It never hurts to ask directly for three or more credit references, that is, other firms that already extend credit to the customer. This affords quick, verifiable information and can enhance other information you've gathered. If you check credit through the client company itself, you may or may not get accurate answers to questions. However, the answers to any of them will help to assess a business:

- What is the corporate structure?
- Who are the principals of the company?
- What is the business experience of the principals?
- How long has the company been in this business?
- Who else gives them credit?
- What are the company's total assets?
- What are projected revenues?
- What has been the track record in recent years?

When extending credit, you are not unlike a bank offering a loan. You need to know whether there is a reasonable expectation that you will be paid fully and promptly. Unlike a bank loan department, however, you probably don't have the staff and expertise to fully investigate the situation and assure yourself real guarantees. In other words, checking credit is fine, but it is not a foolproof way to protect against collection problems.

AFTER IT'S OVERDUE—COLLECTION NIGHTMARES

There is still no definitive way to collect. Because going after these accounts necessitates a great deal of assertiveness, it is one of the areas that new business owners find most unpleasant. It often means letters, phone calls, thinly veiled threats, and personal visits. It means a lot of frustration and plenty of dead ends. If you give up, you don't get paid. If you hang on, you spend a lot of time trying to collect, and you irritate those who hate to see you coming. There is no easy way.

In general, the collection route tends to break down into three chronological stages:

- Initial agreements
- Polite reminders
- Aggressive strategies

Initial agreements

Depending on the product or service in question, it may be possible, although time consuming, to work out initial agreements about payment terms before work starts. These usually entail some mutually agreeable payment schedule and can be developed regardless of the size or importance of the customer. They can be particularly useful for customers who have a poor track record of payments.

The problem is that a customer who is slow to pay for work or goods delivered is likely to be just as slow to pay for various parts of the work or goods during the life of the agreement. Consequently, you are in a position of trying to collect for one segment. Your leverage is that the customer may want to see the finished work or product badly enough to make segmented payments in a timely manner. Although the initial agreement may also carry a deadline for final payment (i.e., thirty days after completion), this doesn't mean you avoid delays and excuses.

Such agreements are generally negotiated agreements, and it takes skill to negotiate terms that are mutually agreeable to all parties.

Polite reminders

Polite reminders generally start with follow-up letters and are usually seen as a mild point in the collection chronology. However, even collection letters sap time and energy that could be spent in a more productive way.

You'll need to set up a system for reminding yourself to send the reminder letters. In some businesses, reminder notices are such a constant fact of collection life that you may find you need to invest in computerized equipment or programs that you hadn't anticipated. It

160

isn't very effective to send notices to some customers and not others, or to send them at inconsistent intervals.

These notices must go to the right department and preferably to the right individual in the company from which you wish to collect. That is probably not the individual or department you initially had contact with, so you will need to research the situation (see phone calls below), which adds to your task.

Effective collection letters are much more than a copy of the original invoice with "Payment Overdue" stamped on it. They need to contain a good deal of specific information about the agreement, order, or contract for which payment is due, including:

- A decription of the goods or services involved
- Detail regarding completion date and first invoice
- Detail regarding any related written or oral agreements
- A reply envelope

In addition, you may have to write a personal narrative portion within the collection letter that appeals to your customer's sense of fair play, reputation, or self-interest. Such narratives may require increasing assertiveness as accounts overdue linger on without any attempt at resolution.

Polite written reminders may also be more effective if they are hand carried by messenger, with signed receipt, or mailed with return receipt requested. This customer is then on notice that you are serious, but again, it costs you.

Phone calls also can be polite reminders, and at first glance they seem like a relatively quick and effective way to get attention for overdue accounts. But when you begin making phone calls for collection purposes, you'll immediately find it is not easy.

Typically, you'll make a number of calls before you find anyone who knows about the account. Often that individual isn't likely to be the person with authority to actually pay the account. Or the person with whom you speak may be very well schooled in the "check is in the mail" run-around. His or her easiest tactic may be to agree, apologize profusely, get you off the phone, and, ultimately, do nothing. Then you wait for payment and start all over, with more calls and letters.

Most first-time entrepreneurs are very conscientious about pleasing their clients—even clients who are beginning to look like terminal deadbeats. Nobody likes to be viewed as carping, nagging, or threatening, and when you get to that point, it's easier to attempt collections by an impersonal letter, rather than over the phone.

Aggressive strategies

When accounts become overdue for long periods—generally over ninety days—you may have to resort to aggressive strategies. These are expensive, involving collection agencies and/or lawyers, and they often mean losing customers or clients who feel you are being difficult and heavy-handed.

Aggressive collection strategies become a must for entrepreneurs. You will need to be armed with capital and resources to undertake them. Most new entrepreneurs do not realistically view collection agencies, attorneys, and court costs as part of the predictable cost of being in business.

Collection agencies can take up a great deal of your time. There are many mediocre and poor collection agencies. You'll need to find a good one. Once you think you have, check out its policies and operations:

- Do they charge a flat fee (generally 50 percent)? It is better to use an agency that charges on a sliding scale—typically 33 percent to 50 percent, with the upper ranges for older and smaller accounts that are harder to collect.

- Do they demand a minimum fee if nothing is collected? If so, they may not work very hard to collect on small overdue payments, etc.

- Do they hold partial payments until the account due is paid in full? Partial payments should be treated with the same percentage split between you and the collection agency as with full payment.

- What methods do they use? If they bully and harass, your reputation may be at stake. If they simply make a few phone calls, you could have done that.

Using a collection agency doesn't mean you can forget about the account and go back to work. You may need to send polite reminders to the collection agency! After all, just like your overdue customers, they have to set priorities, and your collection may not be at the top of their list. You'll also want to track your collection agency's success rate. If they are only collecting 25 percent or less or the delinquent accounts, you may be better off on your own.

HASSLING IN THE LEGAL SYSTEM

As you escalate your attempts to collect, you may need to retain an attorney to advise you of how far you can go and to keep you from overstepping the law. Accounts that remain uncollectible make anyone angry. It's tempting to go too far in terms of threats and harrassment. Be careful—the cost of collecting can exceed the payment due.

Here are tyical ways that entrepreneurs who extend credit can find themselves in the midst of legal hassles:

- Bringing suits for reasons other than collecting. A suit that is primarily for revenge and punishment is not a legal proceeding.
- Using overly aggressive collectors. Collectors who overstep their bounds leave the creditor wide open to legal action.
- Filing criminal charges when the debt itself is in dispute. Make sure it is clear there really is payment owed to you.
- Using force in repossessions.
- Invading the debtor's right of privacy in making attempts to get payment.
- Using threats that may be interpreted as extortion or as blackmail.
- Publicly slandering the individual or company that is overdue with its payments.

Once you really decide to "go the limit," that usually means legal limits. When Paul Harrison began his surgical equipment manufacturing and sales firm in Columbus, Ohio, he started with a handshake and a promise from customers. Later, when he had problems collecting on sales contracts, it became apparent that members of his sales force were being too "friendly" about verbal promises of payment. They wanted the sales commissions, so they promised easy payment plans to the clients upon whom they called. Harrison changed that by sending them out with formal documents that constituted written payment agreements.

Still, many payments were painfully slow and were made only after considerable time was spent in writing letters and phoning.

Harrison found himself busy meeting with sales personnel to assess problems, training them in spotting potential nonpayers ahead of time and grilling them about their personal knowledge of what it might take to get a client to pay.

As he reports it: "The whole system of collections was getting big enough that it could have been a separate company. It had its own computer program and filing system; its own form letters and tickler files for phone calls; and it even generated its own personnel problems among my sales force. I was going crazy trying to run a collection company while running a surgical equipment and supply firm."

Finally, large overdue accounts with several clients merited hiring a collection agency and, later, a lawyer. "Now I had to keep track of not only the overdue collections, but also the professionals helping me attempt to get payment."

Harrison retained an attorney on a part-time basis to undertake all major collections work, while still sending the "polite reminders" out of his bookkeeper's office. "We've got a system and the right personnel to handle collections now, but we still collect far less than what is owed to us. The only reason we've been able to develop a stronger collection effort is because the firm has been wildly successful in its product line—way beyond original projections. Otherwise, we could never afford the time or money to collect on overdue accounts."

COLLECTION POLICY CHECKLIST

Some firms can afford to chase after collections; however, many cannot. Those with slim profit margins that do not take these costs into account are likely to suffer. Some collection policy issues to consider when starting your firm include:

- How much capital will be tied up in receivables?
- Will I need to borrow against accounts receivable in order to remain in business or to expand?
- What will be the cost of this borrowing?
- Should I charge interest on past due accounts? What will that do to customer good will?
- What will be the extent of our collections? Do I intend to let go when it means expenditures like attorneys and collection agencies?

164

- Do I need a computerized system to track accounts receivable?
- Who will handle collections? Are these people trained in this area?
- How can I extend enough credit to attract customers without extending too much?
- Who will get credit? Who on the staff will review who gets how much credit?
- Will I do credit checks? How and with which available personnel?
- Do I want to offer discounts as early payment incentives?
- How will I limit problems that cause slow collections due to customers' grievances with products or services?
- Can I get my own house in shape to process orders or give service more quicky, thus speeding up cash flow to its maximum possible amount?
- Should I offer lines of credit to good customers? Who will approve these?
- Should I keep a bad debt reserve account as a way to budget and protect ourselves against problems caused by collection difficulties? If so, how much?

The answers to most of these questions will not come easily. But if they are not asked and answered, your venture risks some unfortunate developments.

CHAPTER 12
Pitfalls With Professional Help

It is always well to moor your ship with two anchors.

—*PUBLIUS SYRUS*

The biggest problem faced by entrepreneurs when using professional advisers is not retaining them early enough in the business planning process. I have found that most consultants, lawyers, and accountants who promote themselves as assisting small businesses do a fairly reasonable job in steering the entrepreneur past some of the obstacles to getting started. Numerous groups such as the Small Business Administration, local chambers of commerce, and university business departments can assist you in identifying the right professionals.

Still, in the course of retaining professional help, you are bound to face a variety of hazards. This chapter will focus on not so obvious but nevertheless prevalent pitfalls in using professional help.

FAMILIAR ADVICE

Throughout this book, and undoubtedly from other sources, you are frequently advised to seek outside help in addressing certain company issues and problems. Retain a lawyer. Hire a consultant. Call in an accountant. Contact a public relations firm. Professionals outside your company can offer expertise and objectivity in a wide variety of situations—from solving specific and immediate problems to on going consultations and advice.

However, the mere fact of being an outside professional by no means guarantees that someone can really help you. There can be problems in using outside professional help that result in more harm than good for your company. We would all like to feel that once we put ourselves in the hands of an "expert," we can relax and watch our problems disappear. But that isn't always the case. Sometimes, we simply watch our money disappear without an equal effect on the problems being addressed. You must clearly establish at the outset the basis of a professional's fee and his billing procedures.

The setbacks that can occur with the use of outside professional help range from minor dissatisfactions (i.e., your problems do get solved, but require far more time and money than you had anticipated) to major disasters (i.e., not only do your original problems remain, but new ones have developed because of the work of the outside professional). While there are scores of specific causes for these failures, they generally divide into two broad categories: failures stemming from the outside professional and failures stemming from inside the company relating to the use of the outside professional.

NOT ALWAYS WORTH THEIR PRICE

Consider this: Ten percent of the lawyers (or financial experts, management consultants, public relations agents, etc.) graduated in the bottom ten percent of their classes. All professionals are not equally competent in handling problems within their professional purview. It is relatively easy to hire someone who looks good and speaks well but can't deliver on a substantive basis.

Any professional service provider—lawyer, accountant, management consultant—can be selected for the wrong reasons. Mistakes in selection are a prevalent source of problems for entrepreneurs seeking outside professional help. If you have selected the wrong firm or individual, you cannot expect success when using that professional to solve your company's problems.

One public relations professional advises addressing the selection process seriously: "A fancy audiovisual presentation, a nice brochure, and a meeting with the principals may give you a feel for the organization, but it probably will not give you sufficient information to make a good decision. You need more than a gut reaction."

Professionals you retain may be very competent, but still may not be able to help you—there may not be a correct "fit" between that professional and your organization. Perhaps the professional gives you very low priority among other clients. Or there may be personality conflicts that cause him/her to withdraw consciously from your company.

YOU CAN CREATE YOUR OWN PROBLEMS

If you hire a lawyer, an accountant, or a management consultant but don't supply all the major information needed, you can't expect even the most competent professional to successfully serve you.

Similarly, you may have problems in giving the professional you retain accurate information about the issues you want addressed and the needs you have. This frequently happens when you have an immediate need, such as filing a tax return. Because that matter is so pressing, you hire a professional to do just that job. But probably that professional could serve you better if you asked for a more complete overview of your tax situation that included planning for the future. In most cases, the more the outside professional knows about your firm— including its past history and its goals for the future—the better you will be served.

There are several reasons why entrepreneurs hold back information that could be valuable to the outside professional. One involves the entrepreneur's own sense of power and authority. It is difficult enough to delegate authority to those employees on the inside, much less to someone on the outside. So there is a temptation to hold back and not quite let the outsider "in."

Sometimes the entrepreneur withholds information because of a failure to recognize its value. Frequently, we view professionals as omnipotent. They are experts in areas in which we have little knowledge. They know what to do, and they are hired to use their expertise to help us. It's easy to forget that these individuals can't do their jobs alone. They need your help in learning about the company and becoming familiar with the issues involved. Information that may seem commonplace to the entrepreneur could be a revelation to someone not as familiar with it.

YOUR HIDDEN AGENDA

Rob Barnett started a small candy distribution firm that grew to twenty-six employees in just over a year. By the end of the second year, he hired a management consulting firm to draft a formal employee benefit plan. He was disappointed and even reluctant to pay the consulting firm's final bill when he realized that the plan would cost his company more than he had anticipated. "What I expected from their expertise was some sort of economical plan that would show me where I could save on my benefits package."

Barnett hadn't actually given the firm he hired the assignment of saving money. He had simply asked them to draft a benefit plan, a task that often can result in higher personnel costs. Barnett was doomed for disappointment because of his own "hidden agenda," an idea of desired end results that he did not share with the consultant he hired. This outcome is not uncommon among those who hire consultants and are reluctant to candidly discuss their own objectives (often because they are unclear about what their objectives really are).

WHEN YOU HIRE A LAWYER

New companies often find that the first professional needed is a lawyer. That individual can be invaluable for incorporating and reviewing start-up contracts and can help you with the numerous government regulations that affect your business. But you may soon start wondering if you are getting what you wanted from your attorney. Here are some common problems that can occur.

Careless Selection

Many entrepreneurs exercise little savvy when hiring an attorney, and they don't hire the right person at the right time. Hiring an attorney should be done with as much care as hiring a full-time employee at an upper level. In particular, it is important to find a firm or individual experienced in the kind of work and the kind of problems your firm will encounter.

169

If a lawyer has to spend a lot of time doing homework to become informed about the kind of work your company conducts, then you will be paying for that homework time. If possible, get an attorney who is familiar with the kind of work you do (i.e., light manufacturing, agent services, retailing, wholesaling, etc.) and is experienced in the regulations and legal requirements of that area.

Inadequate attention to your needs

The attorney may have other pressing priorities besides handling your needs. When you phone about your case, you may be asked to speak with someone more junior to the attorney you hired. If it seems as if your case is being neglected, make this known to the attorney you originally retained. You need to ask for status reports. If the situation doesn't improve, you'll have to either get a new attorney and/or report the attorney to the local bar association. If you decide to change attorneys, assuming you're paid up, will your original attorney swiftly surrender the file?

Lawyer's performance is not competent

There are circumstances in which you may decide you just do not have competent legal advice. This realization generally occurs only after something damaging has happened, such as mishandling of your property or money. Your first recourse is to contract the attorney directly. If the matter cannot be resolved between you and him, and you feel you should have some sort of restitution, you must approach the grievance committee of the local bar association. If they determine you are right, and you want to take the matter further, you may have a case for a malpractice suit. If you have been financially victimized by a dishonest attorney, and a court settlement does not fully reimburse you, you can apply to the bar association's client security fund, set up for financial reimbursement to such client victims.

Fees higher than anticipated

The lawyer you first contacted was probably recommended to you as well versed in your legal issues. However, you may find that this expertise is costly and the fee higher than you anticipated.

A lawyer who frequently works with start-up companies will find your needs more routine (and, hopefully, less costly) than one who rarely handles such work. When you think you have identified that firm or individual, you'll need a contract or letter in advance that confirms the basis for calculation of fees for the services to be performed, and an estimate of the time needed to do the job. If you retain an attorney on a regular basis, you must be especially aware of the billing procedures—charges can mount up fast.

Dana Bridges, owner of a clothing store, got the name of a local attorney from a friend who thought the attorney had a pretty good reputation. Bridges was only seeking to have the attorney assist with collections by sending out letters to deadbeats and determining the most appropriate actions.

At the end of the month, none of the long outstanding debts had been paid. However, Bridges got a letter in the mail from the attorney's office and was stunned at the figure he was charged. To send out three letters to three separate businesses, the attorney billed an hour and a half at $120 per hour. To determine other steps to collect the funds, the attorney billed an additional hour and fifteen minutes. Associated expenses came to $33.80. All totaled, Bridges was billed $363.80. He was aghast! Then and there he decided that whenever he retained a professional in the future, he would carefully and critically determine how much he/she charged, the method of billing, and the estimated number of hours or level of effort needed to complete the job.

Crisis Mentality

A common mistake is to use an attorney only in times of immediate need or crisis, such as when you've been summoned by the IRS, a job applicant claims discrimination, or another company is telling your prospects that your products have major hidden flaws. Attorney Mark N. Kaplan advises that companies find an appropriate attorney and then use that person as "an outside lawyer-adviser" to provide ongoing legal advice in advance of crises and for crises avoidance. This practice can save time and money.

Kaplan notes: "Sometimes the chief executive doesn't recognize a growing legal vulnerability, but a good lawyer can detect it and nip it in the bud. . . . Bringing a lawyer into closer contact with the business, discussing new ideas, new projects at their earliest stages, yields the best advice."

Some of the areas in which a lawyer with an ongoing relationship to your company can make a difference include the following: timing expenditures to take advantage of tax benefits, negotiating tricky deals with other companies, reviewing the legal implications of major complaints, and advising against practices that could leave the company vulnerable to lawsuits.

The lawyer who works closely with a company on an ongoing basis still needs continual and accurate information to be of greatest benefit. "Avoid the ostrich syndrome in dealing with a lawyer," Kaplan warns, "hoping that if the company doesn't reveal all the information, the truth won't come out. Keep the lawyer well prepared."

WHEN YOU HIRE AN ACCOUNTANT

Dwight Sparks decided to hire B&B Accounting, the best known firm in his area, to deal with all his tax issues for his new commercial carpeting company. He was pleased when one of the B&B founding partners took an active role in setting up the tax files and preparing his first returns. The following year, B&B's fees increased, but their service to Sparks declined. A new accountant was put in charge of the Sparks account. Forms for the second tax year were late and inaccurate. Sparks and several employees spent hours of overtime pinpointing the inaccuracies and working with B&B on the necessary changes.

When Sparks tried to contact the B&B partner who had originally assisted him, his phone calls went unreturned until finally an assistant called back. Although the explanation was "a busy time of year," Sparks accurately assessed that his firm had only interested B&B while a new client. Says Sparks, "They were so attentive, I had no reason to suspect that the next year would be different. Because I trusted them after the first year track record, I ended up with a bigger mess than I might have had if I'd gone to a firm with only half the reputation they have."

Sparks was the victim of a classic mismatch between a company and the outside professional firm it hired. After the initial new client enthusiasm, some large-volume accounting firms lose interest in a small company, especially a company with routine annual needs. Thus, the small client may find he is a much lower priority than the clients who represent large accounts.

Like lawyers, accountants can provide valuable resources. For the maximum benefit, you need to call upon one at the very earliest stages of getting your company off the ground. As with lawyers and all other professionals, you must understand the intricacies of how fees for services are determined and how the accountant will bill you. Typically, entrepreneurs think of accountants as tax preparers and only contact them when some tax crisis is occurring, or when told to by a banker, lawyer, or other counselor.

Your accountant should be selected, retained, and thoroughly advised on taxes well before it is time to prepare tax forms. A good accountant should be able to help with internal accounting, auditing, and financial management issues. If you find that your accountant is not willing or able to do these things, you probably have retained an accountant who lacks the competence or experience you need.

In many respects, hiring and using an accountant for your company is not very different from hiring and using an accountant for your personal finances. You must be willing and available to work with the accountant and to provide information that *you* may not think important. You cannot get the most from your accountant by simply opening up the books and saying, "It's all here; see you later."

A similar problem occurs when filing tax returns. An IRS tax-law specialist says: "The biggest mistake people make in dealing with the professionals they hire to work on their tax returns is to drop everything in the professional's lap and walk away, trusting him to fill out the return correctly and completely, save every dollar possible, and make sure the return isn't audited."

Another common pitfall in using accountants is underuse. A good accountant, on retainer, can find a variety of ways to save you time and money. For example, an accountant can be used to check inventory and inventory controls. If she sees that you are keeping too much inventory too long, resulting in costly storage, she should be able to show you how much you could save by limiting your stockpile of inventory.

Accountants can provide a useful service in reviewing internal financial controls. For example, if he finds that the same person is approving contracts, contract payments, and delivery (see Chapter 8, Cost and Operation Control), he may want to suggest a system that provides more certain internal controls and guards against errors and dishonesty.

WHEN YOU HIRE A MANAGEMENT CONSULTANT

I have found that most entrepreneurs make fairly good choices when retaining management consultants for assistance during business start-up. However, there are numerous ways management consultants can be used throughout the life of the business. Because management consulting firms specialize in a wide variety of areas, their services can be more difficult to use effectively than those of other professionals.

The pitfalls that can occur when you decide to hire a management consultant often relate to misinterpretations of what the consultant can do for you or of what you want to accomplish. Some common problems that occur in hiring and using a management consultant include:

- Failure to accurately identify the problem or need
- Failure to determine whether and how the problem could be solved internally
- Inability to determine what kind of consultant is needed
- Lack of procedures to oversee the consultant's performance
- Failure to work with the consultant in a manner that gets the most from his or her advice

A common mistake is to use management consultants on problems that could and/or should be solved internally. Consultants are best used when there are real indicators that you need outside assistance; for example, when the real issue can be determined only by an objective examination by someone who is not working for the company; or when the problem has been tackled internally, but without success.

Once you are ready to hire a management consultant, you still have the problem of choosing the one that will be most effective for your needs. There are thirty-five thousand management consulting firms and thousands more individual practitioners in North America. They can be categorized as follows:

- Small firms and individual practitioners. Many are excellent, especially in focus areas such as marketing, sales, personnel administration, accounting systems, material handling, and electronic data processing.
- General management consulting firms. These offer advisory services to top management and in functional areas ranging from energy and environment to budgeting and personnel.
- Full-service management consulting companies. These companies are able to start with advice and carry a program right through implementation, providing an implementation team and follow-through on audit and evaluation services.

174

Some entrepreneurs are seduced by the name and reputation of a big firm, when in fact a smaller, more specialized firm might be better suited. The large, well-known management consulting firms earned their reputations through competently handling large accounts that may not bear much similarity to your needs.

Likewise, you may be tempted to fall into the trap of hiring an individual or firm that worked well for someone else you know. But was the problem similar? As with other professionals, you need to check experience and credentials, and compare those closely to your problems and needs.

Many consultants have earned the designation Certified Management Consultant (C.M.C.) through completing the rigorous qualifying program of the Institute of Management Consultants. The Institute's Code of Professional Conduct is a useful guide in terms of what you should expect of any consultant. The provisions serve as useful guidelines for evaluating a wide variety of professionals and are summarized below:

- The basic obligation of every C.M.C. is to put the interests of clients ahead of his or her own, and to serve them with integrity and competence. The C.M.C. will also be impartial.

- The C.M.C. will guard the confidentiality of all client information. He or she will not take financial gain, or any other kind of advantage, based on inside information. The C.M.C. will not serve two or more competing clients on sensitive problems without obtaining the approval of each client to do so. He or she will also inform the client of any circumstances that might influence his or her judgment or objectivity.

- Before accepting an assignment, the C.M.C. has an obligation to confer with the prospective client in sufficient detail to understand the problem and the scope of study needed to solve it. Such preliminary consultations are conducted confidentially, on terms agreed upon by the client.

- A C.M.C. will accept only those assignments he or she is qualified to perform and which will provide real benefit to the client. But the C.M.C. will not guarantee any specific result, such as the amount of cost reduction or profit increase. The C.M.C. will present qualifications only on the basis of competence and experience. He or she will perform each assignment on an individual basis, and will develop recommendations specifically for the practical solution of each client problem.

- Whenever feasible, the C.M.C. will agree with the client in advance on the fee or fee basis for an assignment. He or she will not accept remuneration from others, or make payment to others, on any basis that might compromise his objectivity or professional independence.

Once you've narrowed down the field, you'll need to interview the individual(s) who would actually work with your company. That session should allow you to answer the following questions:

- What have the firm and relevant individuals successfully completed that is similar to your needs?
- What are the backgrounds and consulting experiences of key staff members?
- What types of companies are clients of this firm?
- Does the firm have repeat business with its clients?
- Who in the firm will spend time on your assignment?
- Do the individuals involved seem to understand and take a genuine interest in your needs?
- What reputation does the firm have among other companies?
- Are the fees reasonable and will all fees be clear in advance?
- Will you get a written proposal that covers all phases of the firm's work?

If the firm sounds good and you like the people involved, you will be tempted to hire them on the spot. Don't. As when selecting a computer installation vendor, ask for a written proposal, preferably one that responds to your own written statement of work. That proposal will allow you to clearly see what you can expect and enable you to examine several firms without falling into the trap of comparing apples and oranges. A management-consulting proposal should include the following:

- A definition of the problem
- The objectives, scope, and nature of the engagement
- The areas to be covered by the study

- A recommended program for accomplishing the work
- The general methods to be used
- A statement of personnel who will do the work
- An estimate of the time necessary to complete the engagement, by *task*
- An estimate of professional fees
- A description of the method of billing

WORKABLE PROCEDURES

Some entrepreneurs are more casual in their working relationships with management consultants than with other outside professionals, especially in terms of documenting what will be done, overseeing the work, and evaluating the results. Yet if these steps are not taken, it is impossible to assure that the consultant is serving your best interests.

Documentation should start with the earliest agreement on assignments, schedules, and fees, and should continue with required reports at certain milestones. Any changes in assignment should be in writing, as should consultant recommendations. You have responsibility for monitoring progress, tracking work schedules and accomplishments. Additionally, you are responsible for seeing that the consultant obtains all necessary information for accomplishing the assignment.

According to Philip W. Shay, author of *How to Get the Best Results from Management Consultants* (Association of Consulting Management Firms, 1974), "It is vital not to withhold information or opinions in the hope of getting a more objective result from the consultant. If you have selected the right consultant for the job, he or she will be equipped to make critical use of information from whatever source."

Consider the case of an independent consultant who was asked by the president of an advertising and communications firm to examine overlap and redundancy in various jobs and position descriptions. When she was working from the files on written descriptions, she made substantial progress. But when she began to talk to the twenty-eight employees during desk audits of their positions, she got nowhere.

Nobody seemed to be willing or able to talk about what their jobs really entailed, and it was difficult to determine overlapping responsibility. When she discussed this with the president, a memo was sent asking employees to cooperate, but to no avail. Hours and hours of work resulted in no progress.

At the root of the problem was the issue of trust. Since employees had never been consulted or even told beforehand that a management consultant was hired, they thought of dozens of reasons why they should be defensive (i.e., "Maybe they are going to cut jobs. Maybe they are going to cut pay. Maybe heads are going to roll."). Without management support that extended right down to paving the way with other employees, the consultant could not be expected to succeed.

Before you hire any professional, you must make sure that you and your key staff understand your objectives, problems, and needs.

CHAPTER 13
Marketing Mania

Better to master one mountain than a thousand foot-hills.

—WILLIAM ARTHUR WARD

The information you'll need to effectively market your business must be gathered far in advance of the start of the business, and more appropriately should occur at the same time in which you are contemplating *whether you will* start a business. Your capability to accurately profile your target market and to gauge which measures to employ to reach the market is part and parcel of your decision to even go into business. Peter Drucker observes that of all the elements that make up a business, *customers* is the only one that is essential.

DIVING IN WITHOUT LOOKING

Ralph Abbott had been working feverishly in order that his wine, cheese, and gourmet food store would open on schedule. The store is located in the Wellington Plaza shopping area, a medium-sized, convenience goods, open-air mall. The plaza has four customer entryways. Ralph's shop is located directly to the left of the second most prominent, visible entryway.

The two anchor stores within the plaza are a small Grand Union supermarket and a national chain drugstore. Far in advance of the site selection, Ralph was able to obtain pedestrian and vehicular traffic counts. He felt reasonably sure that the chosen location could support his new venture.

Seeking to appeal to an upscale clientele, Ralph called the advertising representative of a stylish, county-focused monthly magazine. Ralph was dazzled by the promotional package that the county magazine sent him. The demographics of their readership were just the kind of people Ralph wanted to reach. The advertising representative with whom he spoke was encouraging.

Ralph was interested in placing a large flashy advertisement during the opening month and, depending on the costs, a second ad the following month. After reviewing the prices for a half-page ad, Ralph was stunned: "It couldn't be that expensive." Nevertheless, Ralph went ahead and committed several thousand dollars to both produce and run an attractive half-page ad for two consecutive months.

Though the cost of these ads nearly consumed Ralph's marketing and promotion budget, Ralph knew that being in business for yourself means taking calculated risks. He further reasoned that these ads would reach the widest number of potential customers and would cause the most immediate impact. Had he instead used the money for handbills, flyers, smaller community shopper ads, and the like, Ralph believed he would have gotten no better response, with a lot more work.

During the grand opening week, sales were encouraging, but not exactly what Ralph had expected. The owners and employees of the other stores in the plaza all made a point of stopping by, and most of them made a purchase. Regular customers of the nearby stores also came by, but in a matter of weeks there was a noticeable decline.

Ralph was diligent in asking customers how they heard about the store and if any saw the ad in the magazine. Virtually everybody who came by did so as a result of their habit of coming to the plaza. Only three people vaguely recalled "seeing something about the store" in some magazine.

The second ad was already slated to run for the following month. Ralph was confident that running ads for two consecutive months would pull in some customers. Still no one seemed to be responding. Sadly, Ralph realized that he had spent a chunk of change without doing enough investigative groundwork.

Later, in conversation with other business owners, Ralph learned that to successfully advertise in the county magazine, one must run consecutive ads for at least six to twelve months for a message to take hold. They all commented that the money could have been spent more wisely on flyers, handbills, and ads in the community shopper—the strategy Ralph had first contemplated, but abandoned.

Weeks passed and Ralph was simply not drawing the number of customers he had hoped for, even in his worst-case projections. It became clear to Ralph that he should have invested several hundred dollars to talk to a marketing consultant months before the grand opening.

IT'S A COMMON TALE

New business owners, be they in retail, construction, wholesale, manufacturing, or services, have a strong tendency early in the life of the business to misallocate and underestimate crucial marketing funds. Many rely on some percentage from a chart or book indicating how much to spend, and expect that that will do the job. The major error in this approach is that it does not reflect the prevailing environment and any unique circumstances.

For example, the size of Ralph's trade radius, the number of people who could reasonably be expected to patronize his shop, would be equal to the size of the Wellington Plaza trade radius. The number of people residing in the Wellington Plaza trade radius is largely an established figure. Both the plaza supermarket and the drugstore had already obtained or compiled this data. For the sake of example, let's say that the trade radius extends for two and a half miles to the south, one and a half miles east, one mile north and, because of a river, only a quarter mile to the west.

The number of households in this trade radius represents less than one percent of the number of households reached by the county magazine. In essence, 99 percent of the cost of Ralph's ads was dissipated among readers who could not be expected to respond, even if they: (1) saw the ad, (2) read it, (3) were interested in what was being offered, (4) clipped the ad or made a mental note, and (5) actually drove in that direction.

Sound planning is required to identify the most appropriate publications, promotional vehicles, and other marketing strategies to promote a business.

Could a good advertising agent design a campaign that does the job? No, for many reasons. First, advertising agents derive their revenues as a percentage of how much you spend. Therefore, they are inclined to favor expensive ads. Second, the advertising agent is media focused—his natural, and understandable, response to promoting a business is via print media, radio, and television. Depending on the type of business you are contemplating starting, this is tantamount to swatting a fly with a cannonball, and missing.

Effective marketing and promotion consultants can certainly help. Yet there is no substitute for your own clear and accurate understanding of the target and the various resources and vehicles available for reaching the market.

You must develop a detailed profile of your ideal prospect. Stated differently, unless you can describe to a "T" who your typical buyers/customers/clients/prospects are, and their ages, incomes, family status, occupations, dwellings, and so on, you haven't done the job. Then, you must obtain all media rate cards and cost information so that this information can be integrated into your overall marketing plan.

ALL THINGS TO ALL CUSTOMERS

One of the greatest pitfalls facing entrepreneurs is developing the mindset "I already know who my customers are." Once this notion takes hold, the possibility of accurately defining, tracking, redefining, and retracking the target market is severely hampered.

For those serving industry, there are questions that must be answered. What is the nature of the industry that you serve? How big is this industry? How many firms are in this industry? What are the operating characteristics? What are the trends? What channels of distribution are necessary to reach the market?

If you have gathered all of this information, then there are more questions that need to be answered. These concern the buying habits of industrial representatives and agents. What are their reasons for buying? When do they buy? What types of delivery and service do they expect? What type of quality and quality control do they expect?

TAKING ON ALL CUSTOMERS

There is a strong tendency among first-time entrepreneurs to take all business that comes their way, for fear that they will suffer a poor sales period, too much down time, or slack production capacity. Have you ever heard the expression "He jumped on his horse and rode off in all directions"? This pretty much typifies many entrepreneurs' approaches to marketing. As we will discuss in the next chapter, other than in the retailing business, there usually are certain types of customers or clients who you would be better off not serving.

Suppose you are a sales trainer. You are going to start your own sales training firm and there are four distinct markets that need your services. Market A represents the corporate world of large organizations, Market B consists of small to medium-sized firms. Market C consists of independent sales representatives and agents. Market D is the international market. You have studied the situation and found that all four represent potentially lucrative markets. You are well qualified to offer training seminars to any of the four markets.

What, then, is the most appropriate strategy in this situation? Unfortunately, the would-be entrepreneur is apt to formulate a strategy that involves marketing to all four markets.

John Rapp couldn't decide whether to focus on developing his export consulting business or to concentrate on his custom clearance services, which involved helping people expedite goods through customs. Though seemingly related, each required a different focus and served a different market. Not able to choose between them, John decided to offer both. Consequently, his revenues from each remain marginal.

Only by establishing a niche within a specific target market, working from that base, and becoming highly visible, can you hope to successfully penetrate the other markets. To do otherwise is a marketing mistake of major proportions.

The best strategy is to pick the single market that you can most readily, profitably serve, and to stay with that one. When you are well entrenched and have established an outstanding reputation, you can formulate a strategy to tap other markets.

Similarly, if you offer products or services E, F, G, and H, the optimum strategy is to go with the one product or service that you can most readily and profitably offer. For some reason, entrepreneurs are prone to dilute, rather than concentrate, their efforts in target marketing, and in product and service offerings. This dilution phenomenon is so widespread that I am no longer shocked when a would-be entrepreneur shows me six versions of his brochure, for the six markets he will be serving. You laugh! But it happens.

Many entrepreneurs maintain the notion that no single target market, however large and well defined, will be sufficient in size and scope to fully engage them. Thus, they can be found year in and year out scattering their seeds all over creation because of the fear of committing themselves to a target market (or product or service). Does this show an underlying fear of failure or a strong desire to have several escape routes?

When penetrating a marketing niche it pays to concentrate on that niche. Robert Allen, author of the popular books all published by Simon and Schuster including *Nothing Down*, (revised 1984) *Creating Wealth* (1986), and *The Challenge* (1987), advises that, contrary to the old maxim, in order to create wealth, you must indeed "put all your eggs in one basket."

Further Reading on Marketing and Marketing Plans

Connor, Jr., Richard A. and Jeffrey P. Davidson, *Getting New Clients*, New York, NY: John Wiley & Sons, 1987.

Connor, Jr., Richard A. and Jeffrey P. Davidson, *Marketing Your Consulting and Professional Services*, New York, NY: John Wiley & Sons, 1985.

Davidson, Jeffrey P., *Marketing to the Fortune 500*, Homewood, IL: Dow Jones-Irwin, 1987.

Husack, Glen A. and Gordan P. Kraemer, *Do-It-Yourself Marketing Plan*, Buffalo, NY: The Institute for Small Business, 1982.

Kotler, Philip, *Marketing for Nonprofit Organization*, Englewood Cliffs, NJ: Prentice-Hall, 1982.

Luther, William, *The Marketing Plan*, New York, NY: AMACOM, 1982.

Marks, Mary, *Marketing With Facts*, Washington, D.C., Price Waterhouse, 1986.

Quagliaroli, John A., *How to Write a Marketing Plan*, Tarrytown, NY: The Center for Entrepreneurial Management, 1979.

Rapp, Stann and Tom Collins, *Maxi-Marketing*, New York, NY: McGraw-Hill, 1986.

Stanford, Melvin J., *New Enterprise Management*. Englewood Cliffs, NJ: Prentice-Hall, 1982.

THE 18- AND 27-MONTH CYCLES

Now, on to an important marketing secret that most start-up entrepreneurs never seem to learn. For nonretailers, and particularly for those who generate revenues based on contracts or accounts (as opposed to over-the-counter sales), there is an eighteen-month cycle with which you must be intimately familiar. From the time you first make contact with a prospective client to the time you actually do business can easily run to eighteen months. This is much longer than the two to six months most people expect it should take.

If you question that the eighteen-month cycle is accurate, ask your Uncle Joe, who sells machine parts to manufacturers, or your friend Sally, who heads her own management consulting firm, or anyone else who has been in business longer than a few months. Acknowledging the eighteen-month cycle means making many prospecting calls as early as possible and establishing relationships that may not bear fruit until the end of the year or the middle of the next year.

Those in the first year of business have already experienced the sickening feeling of not meeting projections, not having the phone ring too often, and wondering why they are not in demand. But be comforted. Even if you have been the perfect manager, establishing yourself in a market is a long, arduous process that knows few shortcuts. Your ability to press the flesh, to attend the right meetings, and to be mentioned favorably is predicated on an unceasing marketing effort.

Each time you read about an entrepreneur who made a big score, remember that business journalism rarely succeeds in portraying the hardships that lead to the success covered in the article. Moreover, entrepreneurs successful in the long run are just that, successful in the *long run*. No single contract, no one client, no single "big score" guarantees business success. It is the ability to strategically, relentlessly market to appropriate targets that characterizes the one entrepreneur in twenty who succeeds in the long run.

There is also a twenty-seven-month cycle, I've observed, of which all entrepreneurs should be aware. Approximately twenty-seven months from when you first begin your venture, you will be at that stage, revenue figure, or volume of gross billings, that you thought you would achieve in the first six to twelve months.

Remembering Sheldon's Three Times Law, on the average it takes three times longer than you think to get where you want to be. Now, many entrepreneurs are quick to say "Our projections and forecasts are already very conservative." My point is that it takes three times longer than that.

WHO WILL DO THE SELLING?

If you are a people person, if you have a natural flair for marketing, and if you love the challenge of generating new business, then thank your lucky stars. Among entrepreneurs, you are in a select group of no more than 10 percent to 15 percent of the total. For the majority, marketing, and particularly face to face selling, is something that does not come naturally. Many professional service providers, such as consultants, accountants, and engineers, maintain a distinct distaste for marketing and wish the world was structured such that it wasn't necessary. This phenomenon is well documented in *Getting New Clients*, by Connor and Davidson (John Wiley & Sons, 1987).

To be an entrepreneur is to be a salesperson. Winners know how to sell. Below is a list of some good books on selling, which, in your case, is must reading. Even sales representatives earning $250,000 a year recognize the need to regularly read books on selling. Why? Because we all seem to fall back into unproductive patterns so easily.

Good Books on Selling

Alessandra, Tony and Phil Wexler, *Non-Manipulative Selling*, Englewood Cliffs, NJ: Prentice-Hall, 1975.

Boyan, Lee, *Successful Cold Call Selling*, New York: AMACOM, 1983.
Connor, Tim, *The Soft Sell*, Crofton, MD: TR Training Associates, 1981.

Gandolfo, Joe with Robert Shook, *How to Make Big Money Selling*, New York: Harper & Row, 1982.

Girard, Joe, *How to Sell Anything to Anybody*, New York: Warner Books, 1977.

In your venture, will you be entirely responsible for sales? Or will you retain additional sales help? Even if you are able to select the best possible people to support you, some type of sales training must be supplied. Most entrepreneurs don't want to take the time and effort to train someone who may end up working for someone else or for themselves. If your strategy is to hire those already skilled in selling, they may seek a higher wage or commission. Regardless, you must be committed to developing a professional sales staff.

At a minimum you will need to acquaint your sales reps with your company history, background, and the policies and procedures that you have established. Obviously, sales reps must be thoroughly familiar with the products or services that you offer, the materials used in their production, certain design features, and performance capabilities.

In counseling your sales staff, you must focus on your target market, who they are, where they are located, and what their needs are. In addition you must also cover the basic components of prospecting, appropriate terminology, handling objections, listening, closing, and following up. This is no small order. Depending on your type of business, and the product or service you will be offering, you may also need to impart to your sales staff information on:

- Representing you at presentations
- Relaying information to customers
- Handling customer inquiries
- Finding new applications for existing products/services
- Finding new ways to satisfy customers' needs
- Providing marketing information and feedback to you
- Negotiating
- Providing training to customers
- Collecting on accounts payable
- Handling customer complaints
- Maintaining good customer relations
- Scouting the competition
- Maintaining visibility with selected targets
- Maintaining your chosen business image
- And last, but certainly not least, effectively representing your company at all times

To arm your sales staff with the type of information they will need to be successful in the field, you must also impart information about the products and services of competitors and why yours are superior.

Even after providing substantial training and committing lots of time and energy to your sales staff, it still will be necessary for you to determine if their time is being allocated effectively, if their behavior is changing based on customer feedback, and if they are delivering your intended message consistently.

NO TIME, NO MONEY

In the first chapter we spoke about the entrepreneur who is functionally or technically competent in producing the product or offering the service for which he/she wishes to create a business. However, being a good business manager requires handling all of the vital components of the business including marketing.

If you are among those entrepreneurs who do not have a flair for marketing, you are in danger of not allocating enough time and resources to it, beyond what has already been discussed. For independent entrepreneurs, I have found that a *minimum* of sixteen hours per week must be devoted to marketing in the first year.

Harold Wilson left his job as a dietitian to start his own venture selling a home water purification device. Because of Harold's broad background in nutrition and his orientation toward health, it is easy to understand why he was attracted to a miraculous little device that assured people that they were getting clean, pure water.

In many ways, Harold was an ideal candidate to offer such a product, except for one thing—Harold did not like to make new sales calls. With people he already knew, or in those situations where he was simply asked what he did for a living, Harold was just fine. But the thought of devoting twenty-five to thirty hours a week to prospecting made him shudder.

Semiconsciously, Harold devised every task he could to avoid making new calls. He studied the product in further detail. He studied the products of competitors. He organized and reorganized his office. He bought a small computer and accounting software. He developed an attractive brochure. He even hired a part-time receptionist/helper to handle inquiries. In short, he did everything except allocate a significant portion of his time each week to call on prospects. Soon, an odd situation occurred. Harold had no new customers, and paradoxically, no time to sell.

When I first began working with Harold, he wanted to know if he was spending enough time each week on marketing. After I listened to the long explantion of his current activities, I told him that he would have to spend between twenty-five hours and thirty hours a week calling on new customers. Harold accepted this information like a good soldier, because on some level I guess he already knew he would have to face up to that marketing task.

You may not be nearly as reticent as Harold to engage in marketing activities. Yet, the busy entrepreneur—and show me one who is not busy—is apt to roll back the marketing effort because: (1) marketing is hard work, (2) a long time is often required for results to be achieved, and (3) there is false hope that customers or clients will beat a path to his/her door.

Earlier in the chapter we talked about Ralph, who had underestimated the funds necessary to launch and sustain an effective market campaign. Now the bad news: Marketing costs don't diminish over time. That Yellow Pages ad, those brochures, the business cards, the spec sheets, all of the marketing literature, and all of the vehicles that get you up and running need to be constantly replaced, updated, revised, and sometimes scrapped.

Particularly in the case of a restricted cash flow, marketing expenditures are often the item that gets shortchanged. And why not? If you have $800 in available cash and you are facing a heating bill of $246, accounts payable of $415, employee wages of $192, and the need for a new flyer, for a minimum of $650, which expenditure will be made last? Time and time again marketing expenditures rank fourth on a list of four items, or tenth on a list of ten items.

You need to spend a lot to make a lot more. Sure, if your revenue projections hold up, you would have enough money in the kitty for needed marketing expenditures. However, the revenue projections may not be met and you will have to make some cuts. Marketing is bound to suffer.

ARMCHAIR MARKET ANALYSIS AND WHY IT IS FATAL

Armchair marketing analysis is characterized by entrepreneurs who no longer scout the competition, don't continuously examine trends in the marketplace, fail to keep close tabs on their customers (or worse, don't listen to staff who do). The armchair market analyst develops, or more accurately, maintains, strategy based on what happened in the past, hunches, and best estimates.

All of these "techniques" have their place, I suppose, but individually or collectively none are a substitute for accurate, reliable, timely data regarding what is occurring in the marketplace *now*. This problem is particularly insidious for those entrepreneurs who have achieved some measure of success because complacency can set in so quickly.

A RAGING BATTLE

Those who win on the marketing front recognize early that marketing management is a never-ending battle that requires constant attention and concern.

Those effective in marketing realize that no one marketing tool, or marketing strategy, over time is sufficient to continue to effectively attract the desired target market. Sound marketing management requires continuous honing, modifying, and readjusting to the environment and the needs of the desired niche. What worked yesterday may work today but not tomorrow.

Good marketers are forever seeking feedback: What attracted the customer or client? What seemed to be the most effective promotional vehicle? What are the successful firms in my industry doing? Attracting profitable new customers or clients and repeat business is a challenge that never subsides.

CHAPTER 14

For Contractors Only

Habit, if not resisted, becomes necessity.
—ST. AUGUSTINE

If a major portion of your revenue is generated as a result of contracts won through bidding or by preparing proposals, then this chapter is "must" reading. In it, we will review land mines on which contractors commonly stumble and that have lead to heavy strains on the business, disastrous losses, and in some cases bankruptcy. The following will be a bit more technical to reflect the special needs of contractors.

Whether you produce microchips for Silicone Valley firms, adhesives and caulking for plumbing supply distributors, or product test results for the Consumer Safety Commission, you are in a very sophisticated business if your business generates revenues through contracting.

Requests for proposals (RFPs) and invitations for bids (IFBs) issued by large corporations, the federal government, and other organizations and institutions require great attention to detail. The unseasoned entrepreneur faces eight basic ways to go wrong when trying to compete in the contracting game.

1. **Not closely reading all parts of the solicitation.** A Texas manufacturer was awarded a $335,000 contract to supply parts for aircraft flight-recording instruments. After a significant portion of the work had commenced, and sample items were submitted to the contracting organization's representative, it was determined that a specified material had not been used in the manufacturing process, probably due to the entrepreneur's failure to read and follow the very precise specifications.

Understandably, the entrepreneur was upset. He had already committed several tens of thousands of dollars to the project and was in midproduction when the error was first identified. The entrepreneur sought to have this particular specification waived, which, in some instances, is a possibility. However, on this particular contract, a waiver could not be granted because the material used by the entrepreneur did not provide the same level of long-term reliability.

In addition to losses in time and materials, as well as underused production capabilities, the entrepreneur also incurred legal expenses, additional administrative expense, and one long headache. Weeks turned into months before the matter was only semisatisfactorily resolved.

A Kentucky manufacturer was the winning bidder on a contract to provide parts for shock absorbers used in automobiles. The contract called for several items that were outside the contractor's capability, but which he felt sure were of no consequence to efficient production of the end product. He had successfully produced a similar item a few months earlier and saw no problem in offering what was needed on a new contract, versus what was *actually* requested.

The first shipment was unconditionally rejected. Subsequent discussion between the entrepreneur and the contracting officer resulted in contract termination. Though the entrepreneur's losses were minor compared to the loss that would have occurred without early detection, the entrepreneur also disqualified his company from doing business with the contracting organization. Thus, the incident resulted in a compounded loss.

New bidders must determine *all* that is expected before bidding, and take into account the resources necessary for contract administration, handling extensive documentation, quality-control assurance, and reporting. A government agency's way of doing business, for example, varies considerably from commercial practice.

You also must carefully review all materials contained in a request for proposal or invitation for bid. You must learn purchasing and procurement procedures, specifications, material allocation, delivery and supply expectations, and related matters, for each client. If necessary, obtain appropriate counsel when needed for advice on matters of bidders' rights and obligations, appeal procedures, termination, and default actions.

2. Being overly optimistic in determining the ability to perform tasks and assume risk. Small business entrepreneurs, particularly those seeking a first, major contract, are prone to be overly optimistic in assessing their companies' abilities to meet the requirements of an RFP or IFB, and in assessing the possibility of things going wrong.

Sometimes, in an attempt to achieve a certain sales volume or profit level, entrepreneurs effectively blind themselves to the realities of handling new or large contracts. One Norfolk, Virginia, contractor to the Navy was caught in a disastrous financial crunch when his suppliers failed to deliver on time and no backup suppliers had been identified. Delay in the receipt of goods and supplies from other vendors or subcontractors routinely causes a prime contractor to be late in production and delivery, which may result in termination of the contract.

Cash flow represents another problem area for overly optimistic entrepreneurs. Handling a large contract requires raw materials and increased labor expenditures. The inability to maintain a favorable working capital position has been the downfall of many small businesses, just at that moment in which they were about to "break into the big time" and deliver on a number of unprecedented large contracts. The Small Business Administration offers the following questions to critically approach each solicitation:

- Is my staff competent to handle this job?
- Is additional labor readily available?
- Are my facilities adequate?
- Are my quality control standards and procedures in place and adequate?

- Can I meet all delivery schedules?
- Can I handle this job financially?

Answering those questions honestly will help to reduce excessive zeal in taking on new contracts. Moreover, as standard operating procedure, you develop a realistic approach in determining whether you have the overall capability, both technical and financial, to perform on selected projects. The things that entrepreneurs don't want to think about when preparing a bid are precisely those items that must be addressed to be successful.

3. **Bidding on unreliable purchase descriptions or specifications.** An unsuspecting entrepreneur may be stepping on a land mine if the contracting organization is seeking a new product or service for which no previous contract awards have ever been made. Likewise if the contracting organization seeks modification of existing product or service but has not sufficiently updated its specifications.

For example, you receive a request for a proposal that contains a drawing that is five years old. The last revision was two years ago. The odds are high that the required design involves many changes that are not depicted. Any contractor who doesn't question the contracting officer before preparing a bid is asking for trouble. If the drawing contains numerous footnotes and references, it is a good bet that there will be some peculiarities that should be discussed before a bid is ever made. Veteran contractors can often detect unreliable drawings. First-time entrepreneurs should obtain as much advice and experienced input as possible before preparing a bid.

Similarly, purchase descriptions and specifications may contain ambiguous, confusing, or misleading information. Here is a particularly insidious vendor trap. A revision is made to a specification and the update is: (1) received but not placed in the file with the original RFP or IFB, (2) placed in the file but not acted upon, (3) not received in time to make the necessary changes and still meet the deadline, (4) received after a bid has been made.

Most contracting organizations strive to avoid sending out late announcements, updates, or revisions. But it does happen, and it is the inexperienced entrepreneur who is most likely to suffer the consequences.

Another problem with specifications is the proliferation of different numbering systems for parts. Associations, industries, the Department of Defense, the federal government, and state and local governments may all have different numbering systems for the same items.

What actions can be taken by the entrepreneur who wishes to avoid this pitfall? Whenever needed, or even presumed needed, immediately call for a clarification of unclear drawings, purchasing descriptions, or specifications. Also, be certain that any and all copies of dates of revisions to specifications are obtained and incorporated, before submitting a bid.

4. Bidding on estimations instead of actual cost data. A small tool and die company headquartered outside of Atlanta, finds out the size of a federal contract award received by last year's winner. The president of the company mistakenly believes that by slightly underbidding last year's award price, his firm will be in the best position to win the contract this year.

To simply underbid last year's award-winning price is throwing caution to the wind. Your price may not recapture your costs plus a fair profit. Worse, it may not adequately reflect the scope of effort required on this year's contract.

Another problem occurs when entrepreneurs produce a bid price using historical prices on comparable items rather than using updated market information on the current costs of the items, including materials and components.

Frequently, new or first-time entrepreneurs are so eager to get in on the ground floor with a particular organization that they bid low (planning to merely break even on the first job), hoping that this will lead to others. Often this leads to cataclysmic results. The contract is won, but rather than break even, the business sustains a loss, and in some cases, a significant one. This, coupled with the inability to gain quick, profitable follow-on contracts, leaves many entrepreneurs in a worse situation than if they had not bid in the first place.

I have pointed out these problems to would-be entrepreneurs who've asked: "What about the experience gained in handling the contract, the relationships developed with the contracting organization, and the inside information gained while being close to the customer?" These items are valuable, but not at the cost of losing money on contracts.

The ability to effectively determine costs when preparing bids is a vital skill on the road to successful long-term contracting. Yet many fail to take into consideration one or more of the following factors when determining costs:

- Overhead costs and trends
- Subcontractor and supplier costs

195

- Number of person hours, overtime, and the cost of temporary or part-time workers
- Learning curves for labor and salaried staff
- Material costs and associated trends
- Profit or fee

To be successful, you must prepare cost estimates on a per-bid basis, never relying on previously prepared bids or assuming that standard cost estimates or ballpark figures will be sufficient. *Never* bid on a job for which you cannot make a profit.

5. **Bidding under time pressure.** There are countless horror stories about firms that submitted bids without checking them out thoroughly. A New Jersey construction firm bid on a contract to make repairs to access ramps along the New Jersey Turnpike. Although submitting the bid on schedule, they did not allow enough time to carefully review all of the specifications, one of which required that all welding be done by certified welders.

The firm was successful in winning the contract. In the weeks that followed, when reviewing this specification in detail, they realized their mistake. As structured, the firm was unable to meet the requirements of the contract without subcontracting all the required welding. The subcontract resulted in a whopping increase in costs of almost 20 percent. This resulted in a huge loss on this contract, despite efficient subcontractor performance.

A Wichita, Kansas, contractor in his second year had not taken the time to assemble cost-accounting records in order to accurately determine production costs. Confronted with a short lead time to respond to a solicitation, the entrepreneur decided to "go for it." The firm prepared a quick estimate based on educated guesses, rather than actual data.

Subsequently, they won the award only to experience a large loss as the "educated guess" turned out not to be that educated. Adrenalin was pumping as they were "going for it." Unfortunately, the "it" turned out to be a large, unprofitable contract that severely strained the resources of the firm and threatened its long-term viability.

A relatively minor error in computation, when compounded throughout a bid and then multiplied by production quantities, can spell contractual doom. Often, under a deadline, bidders either forego double-checking computations, hoping everything is correct, or erroneously believe that even if they did make an error someplace, it won't really hurt them.

To be successful in contracting you must develop a system in which quick bid decisions can be made. This can be done by maintaining an adequate bank of relative cost-accounting information, updated on a timely basis; developing a rapid system for retrieving revisions and updated specifications; and establishing criterian to facilitate quick bid/no bid decisions.

A longer-term solution to the problem of bidding under too much time pressure is to maintain long-term monitoring and tracking of significant business opportunities. This sounds like a tall order, but the most successful firms do whatever is necessary to learn of lucrative contracts in advance.

To develop a tracking system you'll have to cultivate key relationships with contracting officers, maintain appropriate industry connections, subscribe to key industry publications, keep an eye on the competition, and anticipate needs—a lot of work!

6. Accepting an unrealistic time frame. Closely related to number five above is the situation in which an entrepreneur knows in advance that the time frame called for in the solicitation is unrealistic. In questioning entrepreneurs who undertook such hazardous work, one is uniformly impressed by the foolish belief that "The deadlines aren't fixed."

Entrepreneurs accept impossible time frame contracts for the same reasons as underbidding, to get a foot in the door. The problem with this strategy, in addition to problems discussed in number four above, is that many fixed-price supply contracts, whether with a corporation or the government, contain a default clause that enables the contracting organization to terminate all or part of the contract if the vendor:

1. Fails to make delivery of the supplies or perform the services within the time frame specified in the contract.
2. Fails to make progress so as to endanger performance of the contract.

When working with the federal government, for example, if you fail to deliver goods on schedule, the government may not only terminate the contract, but may procure services from another contractor. Then you become liable for any excess costs that the government incurs when working with a second vendor.

7. Contracting for Products or Services beyond the state-of-the-

art. Occasionally, corporations or government agencies seek creative and exploratory procurements that are negotiated with performance specifications. End products to such procurements may include prototypes, test and evaluation models.

In the case of a creative or exploratory procurement, you must maintain close contact with the engineer or technical representative of the contracting organization to avoid misconceptions about desired results.

Open communication between the contractor and project engineer is essential, particularly in the case when significant evaluation and testing is required over several months' time. Written monthly reports backed by telephone reports and on-site visits can help insure that a "state-of-the-art" type of project does not meander into one that is *beyond* the state-of-the-art.

Successful entrepreneurs eager to conduct creative and exploratory type projects recognize the need for highly capable, technically oriented staffs who can carefully analyze solicitations to determine if projects are feasible.

8. **Hesitancy to take remedial action.** Helen Newton was president of a small EDP systems installation and software specialist firm located in Pittsburgh. Helen's firm had just won a large contract with the state government to update and revamp the motor vehicle department's system for licenses and registration renewal.

The fourth month into the project, the contracting officer failed to supply information necessary to perform accurate system checks and, moreover, indicated that such information would not be forthcoming. Distraught, Helen's project manager was further told to proceed as scheduled, perform what tests he could, and "not to worry about it."

Not ever having had this sort of situation occur, and not wishing to rock the boat, Helen made the decision to proceed. Months later, Helen's firm incurred substantial losses because the system proved to be faulty. Had the missing information been supplied, as prescribed in the contract, there was little question in Helen's mind that the system would have been up and running with no bugs. As such, the firm incurred substantial legal fees to prove it was not at fault.

Fortunately, many contracts contain provisions for resolving disputes. When dealing with the federal government, for example, a vendor may go to the administrative contracting officer for a ruling. If the vendor doesn't agree with the ruling of the administrative contracting officers, he/she could follow an appeals process.

With private corporations, frequently a contract will contain an arbitration clause that binds both parties to the ruling of the arbitrator. In any case, you must have appropriate legal counsel available from the beginning. It is a necessary cost of being in business.

DIFFERING EXPECTATIONS

In my earlier book, *Marketing Your Consulting and Professional Services* (John Wiley & Sons, 1985), co-authored with Richard A. Connor, Jr., I discuss the difference between A, B, C, and D clients. Most desirable for small business vendors are A and B clients because they have a realistic notion of the situation, often have expanding needs, and are generally good to work with.

C and D clients may pose fee and collection problems, ask you to operate on the edge of your ethics, or can be difficult to work with.

A and B clients have reasonable expectations regarding the results you can perform over a given period of time. While their expectations may be somewhat higher than yours, the two sets of expectations are relatively close and, in time, can merge—a situation wherein both you and the client are happy.

C and D clients generally have high expectations, even after a short time period. The expectation gap, what you can deliver, versus what C and D clients expect, may be large. Unfortunately, the gap may not close—a situation in which both you and the client are unhappy.

How can one avoid the pitfall of contracting with C and D clients? There are several measures that can be taken in advance. First, you'll need to find other vendors or contractors who have done business with the clients or customers on whom you are calling to see what their experiences have been. It is not necessary to call upon direct competitors.

When in contact with a contracting officer, ask to see if the organization has a small business representative, coordinator, or office setup particularly to handle the special needs of smaller firms. Also, you should review the corporation's or organization's literature to see if they have a written or expressed philosophy regarding their relations with vendors. Better organizations often have well-developed policies that serve both them and their product and service suppliers.

A common entrepreneurial pitfall is to continue to serve C and D clients or customers when it is clear that these accounts are more trouble than they are worth. Those who tolerate C and D clients over the long run say, "We can't drop them because we need the business." I say, "Today is the future that you were contemplating three years ago; if you don't take action now, three years from now you will still be working with the same turkeys and having the same complaints."

For every hour you would have worked with a C or D customer, you gain three hours in psychic satisfaction, if you decide not to. More important, you create a clearing in which you can contract with more A and B customers. For utter survival, take on C or D clients. However, short-term or stop-gap measures have a way of becoming standard operating procedure. Beware of developing a climate in which the hardball measure of dropping or, better yet, not even taking on, contracts with problem clients is avoided. This is a serious mistake and one that literally separates the winners from the also-rans.

REVENUE FORECASTING USING THE EXPECTED VALUE CONTRACTS

The typical first-time entrepreneur often does not use appropriate measures to forecast revenue, and worse, does not undertake sufficient steps to ensure that a healthy volume of business is being generated

James Fenley headed a three-person graphics and design firm specializing in corporate accounts. When I met James, his method of revenue forecasting consisted of nothing more than mental recognition of four to five possibilities that loomed somewhere on the horizon at varying dollar figures. His system for revenue forecasting literally was not even roughed out on scratch paper.

Some entrepreneurs prefer not to systematically approach revenue forecasting for fear that the forecast is meager. I say, what better way to clearly indicate the need to present more bids, proposals, and sales pitches to prospective clients and customers?

The most effective way to forecast revenue is to use a method that I call the expected value of contracts. Because effective forecasting is crucial to contractors, I will present an extended explanation of how it's done, the nuances of which you must be aware. This method quickly helps you to pinpoint the need to be bidding on *ten* or *twenty times* (!) the number of contracts on which you are currently bidding. Here is how it works.

Assume the following scenario. You recently started your business, a laboratory supply company. You have identified three contracts to supply instrumentation and other high-ticket items. You believe you have a reasonable chance of winning. Contract A is with Taft Hospital and totals $75,000. Contract B is with Research Labs Unlimited and is for $50,000, and contract C is with the county coroner's office and is for $40,000.

If you were an extreme optimist, your revenue forecast would be $165,000, reflecting the situation in which you won all three contracts. Since that outcome is not likely, further analysis is needed in order to produce a revenue forecast that more closely reflects the dynamics of the marketplace.

Suppose that for Taft Hospital, you know of only two other firms that are bidding on the same contract and you have substantial reason to believe your firm to be far superior to the competitors. On the second contract, with Research Labs Unlimited, you are not sure how many others are bidding on the job. However, you do know that there are at least four or five competitors and you are only in the middle of the pack, having no particular competitive advantage.

On the third potential contract, with the county coroner, you feel you are as good as "wired." Though your company is in a start-up phase, you have already visited there twice, they like you, and they have just about said, "The contract is yours." Now, how does information on these three contracts affect the revenue forecast?

First construct a chart that, to the best of your knowledge, accurately portrays the current situation:

Organization	Size of Contract	Number of Competitors	How You Stand
Taft Hospital	$75,000	2	1st of 3?
Research Labs	$50,000	5	3rd of 6?
County Coroner	$40,000	0	1st of 1?

The potential contract with Taft Hospital totals $75,000 and whoever wins the contract will realize that full amount. The best information you have indicates that you are the leading candidate of three bidding for the job. On the basis of probability you might be inclined to say that you have a 40 or perhaps 50 percent chance of winning the job. As you can quickly see, assigning probabilities is a highly subjective art.

I advocate that you regard your probability of winning to be no more than 30 percent. An even lower figure might just as well suffice. You can never count on having accurate knowledge of the situation—things may change and it is best to be cautious and conservative when forecasting revenue.

For the purposes of this example a 30 percent probability is reasonable. Multiplying this percentage times $75,000, the face amount of the contract, yields an expected value for Taft Hospital of $22,500. More on this shortly.

On the Research Lab Unlimited contract, you could be one of five or even ten firms bidding, and you'd have no apparent advantage. Arithmetically, you might think you have a 10 or 15 percent chance of winning. However, assigning a 5 percent chance, or less, is more realistic. On the Research Lab Unlimited contract the expected value of that particular contract is $50,000 times 5 percent, or $2,500.

On the county coroner contract, you surely understand how the game is played by now. You might be inclined to think that you have a 70 or 80 percent chance of winning what appears to be a contract that is "sewn up." Even under these circumstances, it would be wiser to assign a probability of winning at 50 percent or less. You just never know, and only fools count their chickens before they're hatched. On the third contract, then, the expected value is $20,000 ($40,000 x 50 percent).

Adding the expected value for the three contracts yields a total expected value of contracts of $45,000. Surprise! No single contract equals $45,000, yet to the best of your knowledge and ability, this represents the most appropriate revenue forecast for your firm.

Organization	Size of Contract	Probability of Winning	Expected Value of Contracts
Taft Hospital	$75,000	30%	$22,500
Research Labs	$50,000	5%	$ 2,500
County Coroner	$40,000	50%	$20,000
			$45,000

This example, understandably, has been simple, in that you are a new company with no backlog, you are faced with three new contract possibilities, and you know the approximate number of competitors involved and where you stood among them. Also, the amounts of the contracts are fixed and they will all be awarded within a twelve-month period.

The process works the same whether you are facing three or twenty-three potential contracts and can be staggered over time to reflect different starting dates and different payoffs. The one factor that remains extremely difficult to assess is the probability of winning. In many cases, you will have little or no information as to where you stand. There may be a myriad competitors and your probability may not exceed one percent.

PLAY THE NUMBERS

The expected value of contracts method for revenue forecasting also points out the need to play the numbers game. If you are bidding on a handful of contracts, you've already encountered the pitfall of having to rely too heavily on winning most of the few you bid on. You must bid on many, many contracts, and try to get as much inside information, i.e., where you stand in relation to competitors, as possible.

The more contracts on which you bid, the longer you will be in business. The expected value of contracts method for revenue forecasting works best only when you've made many, many bids. There is no other way.

As time passes and contract awards are made, your forecast begins to change. If you win the county coroner contract for $40,000, the probability is no longer 50 percent, but becomes 100 percent. The expected value of that contract becomes the full $40,000. Your overall expected value of contracts jumps up to $65,000.

Organization	Size of Contract	Probability of Winning	Expected Value of Contracts
Taft Hospital	$75,000	30%	$22,500
Research Labs	$50,000	5%	$ 2,500
County Coroner	$40,000	100%	$40,000
			$65,000

Once it is determined that the Research Labs Unlimited contract went to another firm, your expected value of winning becomes zero and the expected value of the contract also becomes zero. Your revenue forecast then falls to $62,500. Similarly, as you bid on other contracts,

203

and as additional information regarding contracts is obtained, your forecast can be updated.

As was discussed in the previous chapter, and particularly in the case of firms whose revenue is derived through contracts, the eighteen- to twenty-seven-month cycle applies. As a general rule of thumb, the larger the organization, the longer the lead time between when you first make contact and when you are awarded a contract or make a sale and actually begin generating revenue. This cycle is a bone-crusher for first-time entrepreneurs. It's no easy path for seasoned entrepreneurs, either.

The best solutions are to have plenty of start-up capital and have so many irons in the fire that the law of averages demands that some of your bids will win. How many jobs do you have to be bidding on in order for the stars to favor you? To be realistic you should assume it is between ten and twenty times what you are bidding on now. Only then can the expected value of firm contracts approximate the healthy revenue forecasts you are hoping to make a reality.

CHAPTER 15

Reentering the Corporate World?

Experience is what you get when you don't get what you want.

—TOM BOSCH

The notion of reentering the corporate world is absolutely the last thing on the mind of a would-be, gung ho entrepreneur. With all certainty, he is sure that he's bid farewell to the corporate world for all time. However, on the contrary, each year thousands of unsuccessful entrepreneurs try to make their way back to the corporate world.

Gilbert Tweed Associates, a New York–based national executive search firm, analyzed the unsolicited résumés that it received in one year. Of nearly 2,000 résumés, over 33 percent came from people who were "self-employed, consultants, owners of small businesses, and entrepreneurs." These individuals were seeking help in being repositioned back into the corporate world.

A LONELY LIFE

In observing the large number of résumés from entrepreneurs, Lynn Gilbert, president of Gilbert Tweed Associates, commented, "Either they are just not hacking it or they don't like it—to be an entrepreneur is a very lonely life."

Many entrepreneurs whose careers were launched in a corporate environment never contemplated that twelve or twenty-four months down the road they would miss the interpersonal dynamics of the corporate life. To be sure, employees you retain provide a measure of human contact. But the quality and nature of the contact differs vastly from those experiences in the corporate environment. Those who work for you, and must respond to you, often fail to provide the insightful jolts and jangles upon which many entrepreneurial types thrive.

So, whether it be loneliness at the top or business failure, tens of thousands of entrepreneurs seek to reenter the corporate world every year. Most of them thought that they never would. To fully understand a major risk of starting your own operation requires understanding the hardships most people encounter in the attempt to reenter the corporate world.

THE OPPORTUNITY COSTS OF HAVING BEEN AWAY

Eric Wasser graduated from a Boston based college in the early 1970s and worked for three years as a marketing assistant, progressing to marketing manager for Gillette. At age twenty-five he headed to the Midwest with his wife of two years, to become a full-time student in an M.B.A. program.

Following the completion of his M.B.A., the Wassers moved to Michigan, where Eric got a job as the assistant director of marketing for a large pharmaceutical manufacturer. Eric assumed increasing levels of responsibility and met each new challenge with determination and confidence. The Wassers had two children and Eric's wife earned a steady income in the records office of a large suburban hospital.

Though he couldn't say when it began, Eric began contemplating going into business for himself, perhaps producing his own brand of vitamins and selected health foods. His experience in the corporate world was tried and true; he was respected in his field and he had gained key insights as to what makes a product sell.

The Wassers were well off. By age thirty-five, Eric had the funds and mind-set to launch his own venture. Moreover, he had start-up capital to sustain the business for the first eighteen to twenty-four months.

Eric's plan was to produce, package, and distribute a complete line of vitamins and minerals to health food stores and distributors nationwide. Using the tools he had learned as an M.B.A. and the broad-based background he had gained as marketing director for the pharmaceutical corporation, Eric produced what he believed to be an "airtight" business plan that called for achieving a breakeven point eighteen months from start-up. He resigned his position with the pharmaceutical corporation so that he could devote his full time and energies to his new venture.

In the first several months, Eric was experiencing cash flow problems that simply had not been anticipated when preparing the initial business plan. Months passed, and the cash flow problems dragged on.

Without emphasizing the gory details, after thirty-six months, Eric was still having trouble getting his line accepted by major accounts. Many chains and individual stores were already carrying six to eight fiercely competing brands and simply had no additional shelf space for newcomers.

Other problems developed. Eric found Food and Drug Administration and IRS regulations particularly annoying. He regarded many regulations as being in conflict with his quest to be a successful entrepreneur. Employee turnover was a constant headache. The cost of supplies kept going up despite government statistics claiming that inflation was hardly moving. Also Eric was spending less and less time with his family.

Another year dragged by. Though some major sales were made and Eric began to taste the tinges of sweet success, he was still working seventy- and eighty-hour weeks "just to stay above water." Eric's "take home pay" for his efforts over the four years combined, barely exceeded what he made in his last year as a salaried employee. At an hourly rate, his earnings were pitiful.

Approaching forty, Eric acknowledged that in a few more years he could certainly "make a go of it." But he wasn't willing to make the additional investment. While maintaining operations, Eric plotted his corporate comeback. He calculated that it would take him anywhere from four to eight months to land the type of position that he was seeking. He knew his business could sustain him for eight months.

OUT OF SYNC ON THE CORPORATE PATH

Over all those years, through all the expenses that Eric paid, one cost that he had never tabulated was the "opportunity cost" of having been away from the corporate world. This cost includes the experience to be gained had he stayed where he was or moved on to another large corporation, the new contacts he would have made, the salary increases he would have enjoyed, the home life he would have preserved, and the sense of balance he would have maintained.

Sadly, it is only when facing the prospect of reentering the corporate world that the high cost of having been away gets considered. Perhaps the biggest single cost of having been away is that you become out of sync, not only with your peers who have remained, but with those who come up after you and become better positioned to outpace you.

There are many who say that experience as an entrepreneur provides benefits that can be applied in the corporate world. This is true. Accelerated experience as an entrepreneur helps you to learn things you never would have learned and perhaps makes you a better person and in theory, at best, a better manager. However, that is not how your experience is viewed by the human resources division (HRD) of the corporations to whom you will be applying. To understand why this is so, let us first take a look at who works in the corporate HRD.

THE "PEOPLE" DEPARTMENT

By definition, the people who work in these divisions have never worked anywhere but within the corporate environment. They are born, bred, and fully indoctrinated to the corporate lifestyle. To them, there is no other.

Your five years as an entrepreneur of your own firm may as well have been spent in a black hole in space. These folks don't care whether your company was ultra-successful or an abject failure. If your company was successful, here is the kind of dialogue you are likely to encounter:

"Why would you abandon such a successful company?"

"What were your earnings and how could you hope to match them here?"

"How is a position with our corporation consistent with your personal objectives?"

REENTERING THE CORPORATE WORLD
—A GRAPHIC PORTRAYAL—

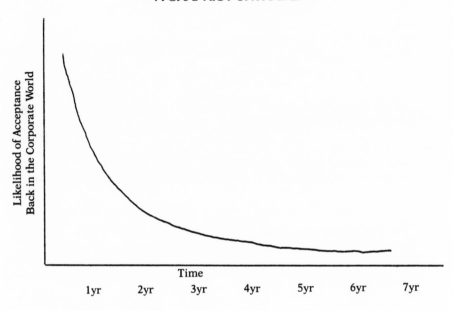

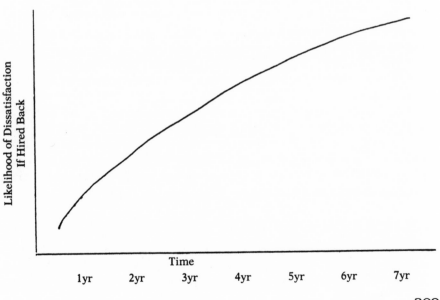

"What role will you continue to play in your entrepreneurial venture?"

"Do you think that you could be happy back in the corporate environment?"

If your business was marginal or failed, here are some questions that will haunt you during corporate interviews:

"How do you think that your experience in the last five years would be of benefit here?"

"What role, if any, are you continuing to play in the business?"

"Why do you want to return to the corporate life?"

"What other ventures, if any, have you initiated or are thinking of initiating?"

'Where do you see yourself in five years? (hint: probably not here)"

"Do you believe you have what it takes to be loyal to the corporation?"

"What made you decide to start your own business?"

"What type of challenge are you seeking with us?"

Your experience as an entrepreneur is going to be the dominant topic of conversation in every interview. There is no graceful way to disguise it on your résumé, on application forms, or in conversation. If your business was successful you will be suspect and if your business was unsuccessful you will be suspect.

The nice folks who staff human resources have never considered leaving the corporate world and launching their own ventures. They are apt to relate to you as somebody just visiting from another planet.

If you don't think the above is true, I challenge you, right now, if employed in the corporate world, to produce a résumé indicating that you have just terminated your own small business enterprise. Then secure a couple of corporate job interviews and see how they turn out. You are not likely to do this, but if so, you would experience the barriers former entrepreneurs encounter.

JUST A PIT STOP TILL YOUR NEXT VENTURE?

Imagine you've convinced the HRD that you really belong back in their organization and can make a solid contribution. Despite the odds against reconnecting with a big company, and in the face of the baby-boom, middle-management squeeze-out phenomenon, it's not impossible to find yourself back in the hallowed halls of big business. Now your own personal dilemma begins.

How long will it be, two years, a year, six months, before what you really want to do—start another new venture—begins to grab hold of you? Here is the question with which you will wrestle: "Is my present position just a pit stop until my next venture?" It will cross your mind, and it may start to wreak havoc on your commitment to your present position and the kind of effort that you claimed you were capable of making.

Ed Milton had successfully made his way back to the corporate world after a three-and-a-half year stint as a full-time entrepreneur. Ed had had it with not meeting payments, promising the world to everyone, and watching his life savings disappear. By the time Ed abandoned his entrepreneurial dream, he was certain there was no way he would ever subject himself to that kind of trauma again.

Yet, a curious thing happened. After four months of working in the Tulsa, Oklahoma, world headquarters of a large petroleum refinery, Ed became itchy to get back into the entrepreneurial game. This time, he reasoned, he was older, wiser, and had a better perspective on what it would take to succeed—all of which was correct. Ed's mental programming became: The nine-to-five job he had landed was nowhere, and running his own show was Valhalla. But he had underestimated the risks, the sacrifices, and the heartbreaks that he would once again incur in business for himself.

As the next few months passed, Ed continued planning his own business. He knew, realistically, that he could not attempt a venture at this point. He lacked the funds to attract any additional seed capital. He figured, though, that in about eight months, by saving everything he could out of his current earnings, and scrimping in other areas of his life, he could get "very close" to being ready.

Ed also determined that by taking care of as much of the preplanning as he could while still fully employed he would be able to "finance" a portion of his new venture while still on the job. Ed progressively expended more of his mental efforts on the new venture and less on his corporate position.

This is not one of those stories with a predictable ending. Perhaps you're thinking that Ed got fired before he was ready to launch the new business; or he launched it while still employed hoping he could handle both for a while until such time as the new business could support him; or he voluntarily left his corporate position and launched the new business prematurely and now finds himself in a struggling position worse than any of his new plans called for.

None of the three situations above reflects what is taking place. Ed is still employed in his corporate position, doing an adequate job, but feels as if he is slowly twisting in the wind. He cannot line up the necessary financing to initiate the new venture. Ed is in a position of extended frustration. He hasn't been able to squirrel away as much as he thought, and he is still recovering from his previous financial debacle, suffered in the throes of his first venture.

Ed's story, and the stories of others like him, is not uncommon. In looking before you leap to start your own business venture, the prospect of failing, returning to the corporate world, and then not fitting in (for whatever reason) usually doesn't loom large in your mind.

WHO PLANS TO FAIL?

If you were to start your own venture, you wouldn't be planning on failing. If you chose to return to the corporate world or the career you had before you became an entrepreneur, you might not have any reason to be concerned about how you would adapt at that juncture. Yet the business world is overpopulated with unsuccessful entrepreneurs caught in a twilight zone of ambition—not able to readily reassimilate, and unsure or unprepared regarding their ability to rescale the entrepreneurial Matterhorn.

BOREDOM STRIKES DEEP

For those who successfully reassimilate and harbor no plans to launch another venture, one still has to overcome personal conflicts regarding previous and present roles. As entrepreneur, you called all the shots and made the big decisions. You put in long hours, often tirelessly, because it was your own venture.

As an employee of someone else, you call a few of the shots at best, make a big decision every once in a while, and get tired sometimes before 5:00 P.M. because it is *their* company. For a while, the regular salary you're paid is very comforting. You can count on it; it pays the bills. Questions you have about your sanity and your ability to meet financial obligations largely subside. But no matter where you land and what challenges you're assigned, compared to the entrepreneurial experience, working for someone else is bound to become boring.

Once you have been an outsider and observed objectively how the corporate game is played, you know that your role can't measure up to the excitement you experienced as an entrepreneur.

PREPARING FOR THAT UNLIKELY DAY

I've asked groups of 100 or more potential entrepreneurs, "How many anticipate ever returning to a previous or similar position in the event the venture fails?" After a few moans and groans and a couple of minutes of discussion on how no one is planning to fail, I ask the question again, phrased a little differently.

"How many can anticipate ever returning to your previous position or previous line of work?" Maybe a few, sheepishly, confess that they "probably could go back" if they "had to," but "it is never going to happen, so why think about it?"

This is an excellent time to return to the discussion in the early chapters. Remember that now perhaps as many as nineteen out of twenty businesses fail, based on a wider, more comprehensive definition of business failure.

What, then, do those nineteen out of twenty people do? Many turn right around and launch some other type of venture, often again under-capitalized or ill-planned. Some retire, some are absorbed into or merged with other small businesses. A small percentage drop out and are never again productive in the business world. A few make it back successfully to the corporate ranks or to a previous career.

ADAPTIVE BEHAVIOR

What are the behaviors and activities of those who are rehired or have reconnected with the employers or institutions that previously em-ployed them?

One activity is to always maintain cordial relations with those for whom you previously worked. That supervisor or that boss you could not wait to leave before you became an entrepreneur becomes one of your greatest allies, assuming you played your cards right, if your venture fails. These are the people you must take to lunch quarterly or semiannually to maintain that human touch. Let them know what you are doing, seek their comments on your operations, and show concern about how they are doing.

Your aim and your focus is becoming successful in the business you have established. To do anything else wouldn't forward your efforts. But maintaining touch with former bosses and employers is a good strategy, whether you ever have to ask a favor of them in the future or not.

Another useful activity is to establish strong relations with creditors and suppliers. Let them get to know you on a more personal basis, and they'll be strong allies when things aren't going according to plan. In a bust situation, they may serve as financial, employment, or referral sources, all of which could come in extremely handy. Other key relationships and individuals to be cultivated include directors and executives of associations in your industry, editors of industry publications, and any other organizations that broadly serve your industry.

As an entrepreneur in a viable business, developing a support network enhances marketing efforts and raises your standing within the industry and the community at large. The added benefit, in the case of a failing business, is that you are more likely to land back on your feet in less time for having kept these key connections and relationships alive. Virtually anyone who can help you in a bust situation can also be of great benefit in general.

MAINTAINING TIES

Jean Kramer worked as a trainer for the Phoenix office of a large EDP manufacturer and distributor. Jean was very good at her job, commanded a healthy salary, and made lots of contacts throughout the mid-Arizona region. The idea of starting her own business offering computer instruction and training was very appealing to her, even though the thought of not receiving a regular paycheck seemed a bit scary.

One afternoon, when things were going particularly well, Jean got a vision of how it could be, and then and there knew that she would be leaving the company to start one of her own. Three months later to the day, when her business cards arrived, Jean gave the company a thirty-day notice and turned her attention toward her new venture.

Though starting with a couple of contracts in hand, Jean quickly found that maintaining a positive cash flow was a difficult task. By the end of the first year, Jean had only made 60 percent of what she had earned as a salaried employee, and that figure was before expenses. In the second year, things picked up a bit as Jean had a fine reputation, and she added an assistant to her company.

All the while, never intending to fail, Jean maintained cordial relations with her previous boss, co-workers, and customers and suppliers whom she had come to know. She was also well connected with the area's civic and professional groups and served as membership chair for one of them.

Though she had landed some new accounts of medium size, the large "bread and butter" accounts that Jean was really seeking kept eluding her. For a variety of reasons, Jean kept losing out to larger, more established training firms.

By the end of the third year, Jean was a marginally successful businesswoman in the community. However, the type of earnings she was seeking simply were not being generated and did not appear to be on the horizon. For months on end, Jean considered the possibility of terminating the business and perhaps returning to the corporate world. Having kept in touch with her previous boss and a crop of professionals from her old company, Jean felt reasonably sure that her return to the corporate world would not require the nightmare effort that others she had heard about experienced.

Does it matter whether Jean continued in her business and perhaps in the fourth and fifth year achieved some of the contract breakthroughs she was seeking, or if she returned to become a trainer within a corporate environment? Not really. Jean did make the choice to return to the corporate world. The fundamental point is this: Jean embarked in business for herself with the same enthusiasm, hopefulness, and desire for great earnings that most other entrepreneurs have. She wasn't planning to fail, or be stuck in a modest-earnings venture. Yet, partly as a function of her style, and because it just made good business sense, Jean took the time to maintain important personal connections within the previous work environment.

Since Jean started a training firm that was an off-shoot of what she had already been doing, it was quite natural for her to maintain these relationships. Yet, many entrepreneurs start new ventures in the same fields in which they were already working and many are eager to burn their bridges—they are disgruntled regarding the way their particular bosses treated them. Some are simply "too busy" and regard this with such little priority that it never gets done.

TODAY'S PIONEERS

By now you might think my thoughts on starting a venture are negative. Surprisingly, nothing could be farther from the truth. After absorbing the information presented, and carefully acknowledging the pitfalls others have experienced (and that you too may experience), if you are still determined to start your own venture, I say proceed!

Enthusiastic, competitive entrepreneurs are today's pioneers, and in many respects exhibit the same courage and fortitude as the pioneers of 140 years ago who opened up the American West, established new frontiers, and made the world a little larger for everyone else. Truly, there are few rewards in life as satisfying as being successful in your own business enterprise.

Considering the odds against the entrepreneur who braves the storm, takes calculated risks, and emerges a winner, this person commands my deep respect and, rightfully, the respect of his/her community. Considering that small businesses create over 80 percent of all new jobs, make substantial research and development breakthroughs, contribute to tax revenues, and strengthen the national economy, successful entrepreneurs can rightly take their place among the heroes from other walks of life.

The value of an idea lies in the using of it.

THOMAS ALVA EDISON

Glossary

Advertising Any paid form of nonpersonal presentation of ideas, goods or services by an identified sponsor. Advertising is the main form of mass selling.

Assets The total of liabilities and net worth or owner's equity. Assets are items that have future use in a business beyond the present accounting period.

Audit An examination of financial statements, underlying data, accounting records, and accounting systems to determine if a company's financial statements are in accordance with generally accepted accounting procedure.

Bankruptcy A legal declaration that a firm is unable to meet its obligations. Can be voluntary, chosen by the individual with financial troubles, or involuntary, initiated by creditors.

Bidding The process of formally indicating interest in contracting with another

217

party to perform a specific task or set of tasks. Generally includes an itemized cost and fee schedule.

Break even analysis An examination of the interrelationships of both fixed and variable costs, volume, and profit.

Break even point The level of sales volume at which revenues equal total costs.

Business cycle A definable pattern of changes in business activity that is periodically repeated. Particular cycles do not correspond to any accounting period.

Business name A registered business name, usually on a "doing business as. . ." (D.B.A.) form with the local government. Part of the business licensing process, preventing any other business from using that same name for a similar business in the same locality.

Business plan The strategy or game plan of a business, includes a review of all its components as a business and their contribution toward company objectives. Future oriented.

Buyer An individual charged with the responsibility for identifying, analyzing, and selecting goods and services.

Capability statement A written description of a business's background, experience, and current activities that demonstrate effectiveness in offering specified goods/services.

Carrying costs Costs associated with holding inventory, such as interest charges or funds invested in inventory; storage and devaluations costs.

Cash A broad classification of easily transferred negotiable assets, such as coin, paper money, checks, money orders, and money on deposit in banks.

Cash cycle The length of time between the purchase of raw materials and the collection of accounts receivable generated in the sale of the final product.

Cash flow The amount of funds received during a given period minus what is paid out during the same period.

Channels of distribution The path that a product of service takes, starting from the manufacturer or supplier to the end user.

Client-centered marketing The continuing process of developing and enhancing advocate-oriented relationships with receptive people who are or can be useful to you in using, retaining, and referring you and your services.

Collections The systematic process of obtaining money due to a business.

Communication Transmitting a message from a sender or source to a receiver.

Consumer market All the individuals and dwelling units who buy or acquire goods and services for personal consumption.

Corporation A legal form of business granted a charter, recognizing it as a separate entity having its own rights, privileges, and liabilities distinct from those of its members.

218

Credit With suppliers, a trade courtesy enabling one to receive goods to be paid for later. With bankers, financial reputation signified by ability to meet obligations.

Credit rating An evaluation of the ability of a business to honor its debts and financial obligations.

Creditor A business or individual to whom a debt is owed.

Customer The only element crucial to the existence of a business. A person or group with potentially unmet needs.

Customer service Satisfying and assisting consumers by various means including offering technical assistance, handling grievances, providing information, and making substitutions.

Direct Mail A form of advertising in which a message is sent to preselected targets.

Discontinuance As used by Dun & Bradstreet, businesses that cease operations for reasons such as loss of capital, inadequate profits, ill health of the entrepreneur, or retirement.

Distribution channel The set of parties assisting in transferring particular goods or services from producer to consumer.

Distributor An element or party in the channel of distribution who transfers items of value between other parties in the channel.

Documentation Written materials that support claims as to specific or general capabilities. May include proofs, photos, testimonials, references, and other supporting evidence.

Down time A disruption in routine operations in which a machine, department, or factory is inactive during normal hours.

Entrepreneur An individual who seizes, conceives of, or converts a product or service that fulfills a need in the marketplace.

Equity The net worth of a business, consisting of capital stocks, capital or paid-in surplus, earned surplus or retained earnings, and possibly certain net worth reserves.

Escrow Placing in the hands of a third party the property, money, or assets of a firm to be released to a grantee only upon the fulfillment of a condition.

Expected value As used in this book, the dollar volume of a contract multiplied by the probability of winning the contract.

Expected value of contracts The sum of the expected value of an array of contracts on which bids or proposals have been submitted.

Exposure Gaining visibility and insights and experience beyond one's immediate working environment, i.e., throughout the entire organization, the community, or the industry.

Factoring A method of financing accounts receivable wherein a firm sells its accounts receivable (generally without recourse) to a financial institution (the factor).

Failure As used by Dun & Bradstreet, businesses that ceased operations: following assignment or bankruptcy; with losses to creditors after foreclosure of attachment; by voluntarily withdrawing, leaving unpaid debts; following court actions such as receivership, reorganization, or arrangement; or by voluntarily compromising with creditors. Note: Failures as defined by Dun & Bradstreet represent only a small percentage of total closings.

Fixed assets Assets or a business that are of a relatively permanent nature and are necessary for functioning, such as buildings, furniture, equipment.

Fixed costs Costs that do not vary with changes in output, such as interest on long-term loans, rents, or salaries.

Forecasting The art of anticipating what amount of revenue will be generated in a given time period. Also what buyers are likely to do under a given set of conditions.

Fortune 500 Major U.S. industrial corporation with sales (in 1985) of over $400,000,000 as tabulated and ranked by *Fortune* magazine.

Franchising Franchising is a form of licensing by which the owner—the franchisor— distributes or markets a product, method, or service identified by a brand name through affiliated dealers (the franchisees), who are given exclusive access to a defined geographical area.

Geographic segmentation Subdividing a market into units such as continents, nations, states, regions, counties, cities, or neighborhoods.

Good faith Acting with a sincere belief that the accomplishment intended is not unlawful or harmful to another.

Good will Intangible assets of a firm established by the amount of the price paid for the going concern above and beyond book value.

IFB Invitation for bid. An announcement received by a product or service vendor from a government agency or organization soliciting a bid for work to be done.

Image The sum total of the perceptions your customers, clients, and all others have about you and your business.

Implied warranty A guarantee arising from contract law that implies that goods for sale are reasonably fit for their ordinary and intended, or particular, purpose.

Inventory The total of items of tangible personal property (1) are held for sale in the ordinary course of business, (2) are in the process of production of goods and services available for sale.

Job cost The aggregate cost of direct labor and material costs and indirect manufacturing expenses associated with a specific order or job.

Job description A written summary of the key components of the tasks, duties, responsibilities, and experiences a candidate should have to successfully handle a given position.

Liability Assets minus net worth or owner's equity. Liabilities are claims against assets by outside parties to the company.

Leveraging The process of identifying and capitalizing on the smallest number of actions that produce the largest number/amount of results.

Line and staff Descriptive terms that define the structure of an organization. Line refers to jobs or roles that have direct authority and responsibility for output, while staff personnel contribute indirectly to production and usually advise line personnel.

Line of credit An arrangement whereby a financial institution commits itself to lend up to a specified maximum amount of funds during a specified period.

Liquidity A measure of a firm's cash position and its ability to meet maturing obligations.

Manager One who "tells people in fairly specific terms what to accomplish and then counsels them to the extent necessary in their efforts to accomplish these objectives."

Market The set of existing and prospective users of a product or service.

Marketing The process of planning and executing the conception, pricing, promotion, and distribution of ideas, goods, and services to create exchanges that satisfy individual and organizational objectives.

Marketing information system A network of people, equipment, and procedures to collect, organize, analyze, evaluate, and distribute timely, relevant, and accurate information used by marketing decision-makers.

Marketing management The analysis, planning, implementation, and control of programs designed to create, build, and maintain mutually beneficial exchanges with target buyers for the purpose of achieving organizational objectives.

Marketing plan The "hard-copy" end-product of the marketing planning process.

Marketing planning The continuing process of: auditing the company and its markets to identify opportunities and problems; establishing priority; setting goals; allocating and organizing resources required to accomplish the goals; and scheduling, doing, and monitoring results.

Marketing research The systematic collection, analysis, and reporting of data to provide information for marketing decision-making.

Marketing strategy The marketing logic by which a business seeks to achieve its marketing objectives.

Marketing segmentation A marketing strategy conceived to produce a product or service that embodies characteristics preferred by a small part of the total market for the product or service.

Market penetration A systematic campaign to increase sales in current markets of an existing product or service.

Market segment A distinct or definable subset of a target market.

Milestones Interim steps toward pursuit of a goal or a project deadline.

Minority businesses Businesses whose owners are deemed, usually based on government-produced criteria, "socially and/or economically disadvantaged."

Motivation Actions within each individual that cause him or her to act.

Networking Interacting with others for the purpose of exchanging information and professional favors.

Net Worth Assets minus liabilities. The portion of a company's assets that can be claimed by owners or investors of the company.

News Release An announcement of community, state, national, or international interest distributed to print media by the organization about whom the release is written.

Niche (marketing niche)—An identifiable market or market segment that can be readily and prosperously penetrated.

Orientation checklist An established system, usually on a preprinted form, for fully acquainting and acclimating a new employee to his or her new position or organizational environment.

Organizational chart A linear direction of responsibility and authority within a company or institution.

Overhead All the costs of business other than direct labor and materials, including such items as maintenance, supervision, utility costs, and depreciation.

Owner's equity Those assets left over after all creditors have been paid off. The two sources of equity are owner investment and prior earnings from profitable operations.

Payback period The length of time required for the net revenues of an investment to return the cost of the investment.

Personal selling A professional marketing effort involving face-to-face communication and feedback, with the goal of making a sale or inducing a favorable attitude toward a company and its product or services.

Physical distribution The tasks involved in planning, implementing, and controlling the physical flows of materials and final goods from points of origin to points of use to meet the needs of customers at a profit.

Procurement A contract award that secures the delivery of specific goods or the performance of specified services.

Product Product or services that can be offered to a market for acquisition, use, consumption, or adoption that satisfies a want or need.

Product differentiation Presenting a product such that it is perceived by customers as unique or somewhat unique from other products available.

Product line A group of products that are closely related because they satisfy a class of needs, are used together, are sold to the same customer groups, are marketed through the same type of outlet, or fall within given price ranges. Also can mean the full range of products marketed by a company.

Product mix The set of all product lines and items that a particular seller offers for sale to buyers.

Productivity Systematic efforts to "increase, extend, or achieve human and organizational benefit outputs and decrease resource inputs."

Pro forma income statement An income statement prepared for a future time period, depicting projected revenues and expenses of operating a business.

Promotion The act of furthering the growth and development of a business by generating exposure of goods or services to a target market.

Proposal A document designed to describe a firm's ability to perform a specific task(s) by indicating that the firm has the facilities, human resources, management experience, and track record to assure successful project performance and completion.

Prospecting Seeking potential buyers or customers; identifying and contacting likely candidates for purchase of your goods or services.

Purchasing agent As used here, a general term connoting any employed individual whose job responsibility involves in some way buying goods and/or services.

Purchasing department That portion of a company charged with the task of buying goods and services; supplies and commodities; and maintenance, repair, and overhaul.

Purchasing manager One who supervises, trains, and develops buyers and assistant purchasing managers, while maintaining some direct buying responsibilities.

Quality control Establishing product or service specifications in regards to performance capability, appearance, durability, etc. The process of insuring that product design or service delivery incorporates predetermined requirements.

Qualified vendor A supplier of goods or services who is able to competently fulfill corporate needs.

Ratio analysis An examination of the relationship of items in financial statements, expressed as ratios or percentages.

Reputation The perception of value and integrity that you've demonstrated in serving your customers.

ROI Return on investment. A measure for determining the profitability achieved as a result of risking something of specific value.

RFP Request for proposal. A document prepared by the federal government or organizations that describes a job or task to be performed and that solicits offers to handle such work.

SBA The U.S. Small Business Administration, an agency of the U.S. government that was created in 1953 to facilitate and promote the growth of the nation's small businesses.

Sales management Operations and activities involved in the planning, directing, and controlling of sales activities.

Sales territories Market allocations based on geography, line of business, or other criteria that facilitates the sales management function.

Selling The exchange of goods, services, or ideas between two parties.

Size standards Measurements of business size that determine whether a business is "small" by the definitions of the Small Business Administration, usually based on its particular type of business and the number of employees or gross annual sales.

Sole source Soliciting and using only one vendor to supply predetermined products or services.

Sourcing As in "identifying new services." Can be for goods/services or the vendor that supplies them.

"Spec" sheets A detailed account of a product's specifications—capabilities, tolerances, performance, materials, etc.

Standard The basic limits or grade ranges in the form of uniform specifications to which particular manufactured goods may conform, and uniform classes into which the products may or must be sorted or assigned.

Standard Industrial Classification (S.I.C.) A U.S. Bureau of the Census classification of industries based on the product produced or operation performed by the industry.

Standardization A process whereby uniformity and conformity is sought.

Statistical process control A quantitative tool for enhancing quality control that relies on probability theory and random sampling techniques.

Supplier One who fulfills product or service needs.

Target market That portion of the total market that a company has selected to serve.

Target marketing Focusing marketing efforts on one or more segments within a total market.

Test marketing Selecting one or more markets in which to introduce a new product or service, and observing and assessing performance and to determine what revisions are needed, if any.

Trade association An organization established to benefit members of the same trade by informing them of issues and developments within the organization and about how changes outside the organization will affect them.

Trade credit Interfirm debt arising through credit sales and recorded as an account receivable by the seller and as an account payable by the buyer.

Trade radius The geographic area in which a business can expect to derive 80 percent of more of its revenues.

Trade show A commercial or industrial gathering over a concentrated time period in which sellers at preassigned stations present goods and services for possible sale to prospective buyers.

Vendor As used here, synonymous with supplier; one who fulfills product or service needs.

Working capital A measure of a firm's short-term assets—cash, short-term securities, accounts receivable, and inventories, and its ability to meet short-term obligations.

Bibliography

Take A Chance to Be First, by Warren Avis. New York: MacMillan Publishing, 1986.

The Job Generation Process, by David L. Birch. Cambridge: MIT Program on Neighborhood and Regional Change, 1979.

Entrepreneurship, by John G. Burch. New York: John Wiley & Sons, 1986.

Consumer and Small Business Bankruptcy: A Complete Working Guide, by William A. Chatterton. Englewood Cliffs, NJ: Institute for Business Planning, 1982.

The Five Deadly Mistakes That Lead to Bankruptcy, by Gene L. Corder. Phoenix: Redcor Book Publishing, 1981.

With No Fear of Failure: Recapturing Your Dreams Through Creative Enterprise, by Tom J. Fatjo, Jr. and Keith Miller. Waco, TX: Word Books, 1981.

Where Have All the Woolly Mammoths Gone?, by Ted Frost. Englewood Cliffs, NJ: Prentice-Hall, 1977.

The E Myth—Why Most Businesses Don't Work and What To Do About It, by Michael E. Gerber. New York: Ballinger, 1985.

How to Save Your Business: Winning Ways to Put Any Financially Troubled Business Together Again, by Arnold S. Goldstein. Wilmington, DE: Enterprise Publishing, 1983.

Starting on a Shoestring, by Arnold S. Goldstein. New York: John Wiley & Sons, 1985.

Small Business Management: Planning and Operation, by William D. Hailes, Jr., and Raymond T. Hubbard. New York: Van Nostrand Reinhold, 1983.

Marketing for Your Growing Business, by Rick S. Haynes and Gregory Elmore. New York: John Wiley & Sons, 1986.

Success and Failure in Small Business, edited by John Lewis, John Stanworth, and Allan Gibb. Brookfield, VT: Gower Publishing, 1984.

Principles of Small Business Management, by William N. MacFarlane. New York: McGraw-Hill, 1977.

How to Start, Finance and Manage Your Own Small Business, by Joseph R. Mancuso. New York: Center for Entrepreneurial Management, 1985.

How to Write a Winning Business Plan, by Joseph R. Mancuso. New York: Center for Entrepreneurial Management, 1985.

Building Your Business Plan, by Harold J. McLaughlin. New York: John Wiley & Sons, 1986.

Why Companies Fail, by Harlan D. Platt. Lexington, MA: Lexington Books, 1985.

Small Business Guide to Borrowing Money, by Richard Rubin and Philip Goldbery. New York: McGraw-Hill, 1980.

Small Is Beautiful: Economics As If People Mattered, by E. F. Schumacher. New York: Harper & Row, 1974.

The Entrepreneurs: Twelve Who Took Risks and Succeeded, by Robert L. Shook. New York: Harper & Row, 1980.

Small Business USA: Small Companies' Role in Sparking America's Economic Transformation, by Steven Solomon. New York: Crown Publishers, 1986.

Entrepreneurship and Small Business Management, by Kenneth R. Van Voorhis. Boston, MA: Allyn and Bacon, 1980.

GOVERNMENT PUBLICATIONS

Current Business Failure Epidemic: Hearing Before the Subcommittees on General Oversight of the Committee on Small Business, Ninety-seventh congress, Second Session, Washington, D.C. June 23, 1982.

Small Business Failures: Hearing Before the Subcommittee on Antitrust and Restraint of Trade Activities Affecting Small Business of the Committee on Small Business, Ninety-seventh Congress, Second Session, New York City, NY, June 25, 1982.

Business Services Directory: Office of Business Liaison, U.S. Department of Commerce, Washington, D.C. 20230.

A Small Business Guide to the FDA: (HHS Pub. No. (FDA) 82–1092), Small Business Representative, Food and Drug Administration, Region III, 900 U.S. Customs House, Philadelphia, PA 19106.

Q&A: Small Business and the SEC: (SEC 1753 92-83), Office of Small Business Policy, U.S. Securities and Exchange Commission, 450 Fifth Street, N.W., Washington, D.C. 20549.

Your Business and the SBA: Public Communications, Small Business Administration, 1441 L Street, N.W., Washington, D.C. 20416.

SBA Veteran's Handbook: Small Business Administration, 1441 L Street, N.W., Washington, D.C. 20416.

Small Business Assistance at the EPA: Small Business Ombudsman, U.S. Environmental Protection Agency, 401 M Street, S.W., Washington, D.C. 20460.

Is Exporting For You?: (GPO 1981–357–559/9983), Public Communications, Small Business Administration, 1441 L Street, N.W., Washington, D.C. 20416.

Doing Business With the Federal Government, and U.S. Government Purchasing and Sales Directory: (DGP 1981 0–355–844 and GPO 045–000–00153–0), U.S. Government Printing Office, North Capitol and H Street, N.W., Washington, D.C. 20401.

Procurement and Technical Assistance: (GPO 1983 0–401–029: QL 3), Office of Procurement and Technical Assistance, Small Business Administration, 1441 L Street, N.W., Washington, D.C. 20416.

SMALL BUSINESS ADMINISTRATION
DISTRICT OFFICES

Alabama
2121 8th Avenue North
Suite 200
Birmingham, AL 35203-2398
(205) 254-1344

Alaska
701 C Street, Box 67
Federal Building Annex
Room 1068
(8th and C, Module G)
Anchorage, AK 99513
(907) 271-4022

Arizona
2005 North Central Avenue
5th Floor
Phoenix, AZ 85004
(602) 261-3732

Arkansas
320 West Capitol Avenue
Suite 601
Little Rock, AR 72201
(501) 378-5871

California
2202 Monterey Street
Suite 108

Fresno, CA 93721
(209) 487-5189
350 South Figueroa Street
Suite 600
Los Angeles, CA 90071
(213) 894-2956
880 Front Street
Federal Building
Suite 4-S-29
San Diego, CA 92188
(714) 293-5430
211 Main Street
Fourth Floor
San Francisco, CA 94105
(415) 974-0649

Colorado
New Custom House Building
721 Nineteenth Street
Fourth Floor
Denver, CO 80202
(303) 844-3984

Connecticut
One Hartford Square, West
Second Floor
Hartford, CT 06106
(203) 722-2511

Delaware
(Branch Office)
844 King Street, Room 5207
Federal Building, Box 16
Wilmington, De 19801
(302) 573-6294

District of Columbia
1111 18th Street, N.W.
Sixth Floor
P.O. Box 19993
Washington, DC 20036
(202) 634-4950

Florida
2222 Ponce de Leon Blvd.
Fifth Floor
Coral Gables, FL 33134
(305) 350-5521
400 West Bay Street
Room 261
Box 35067

229

Jacksonville, FL 32202
(904) 791-3784

Georgia
1720 Peachtree Road, N.W.
Sixth Floor
Atlanta, GA 30309
(404) 881-2441

Hawaii
P.O. Box 50207
300 Ala Moana Blvd.
Room 2213
Honolulu, HI 96850
(808) 546-8950

Idaho
1020 Main Street
Suite 290
Boise, ID 83702
(208) 334-1696

Illinois
219 South Dearborn Street
Room 437
Chicago, IL 60604
(312) 353-4528

Indiana
New Federal Building
Room 578
575 N. Pennsylvania Street
Indianapolis, IN 46204–1584
(317) 269-7272

Iowa
210 Walnut Street
Federal Building, Room 749
Des Moines, IA 50309
(515) 284-4422

373 Collins Road, Northeast
Cedar Rapids, IA 52402
(319) 399-2571

Kansas
Main Place Building
110 East Waterman Street
Wichita, KS 67202
(316) 269-6616

Kentucky
P.O. Box 3517
600 Federal Place, Room 188
Louisville, KY 40201
(502) 582-5971

Louisiana
1661 Canal Street, 2nd Floor
Fisk Federal Building
New Orleans, LA 70112–2890
(504) 589-6685

Maine
40 Western Avenue, Room 512
Augusta, ME 04330
(207) 622-8378

Maryland
10 North Calvert Street
Third Floor
Baltimore, MD 21202
(301) 962-4392

Massachusetts
150 Causeway Street
Tenth Floor Boston, MA 02114
(617) 223-4074

Michigan
477 Michigan Avenue
McNamara Building
Room 515
Detroit, MI 48226
(313) 226-6075

Minnesota
610C Butler Square
100 North Sixth Street
Minneapolis, MN 55403
(612) 349-3550

Mississippi
322 Federal Building
100 West Capitol Street
Jackson, MS 39269
(601) 960-4378

Missouri
Professional Building
Sixth Floor
1103 Grand Avenue

Kansas City, MO 64106
(816) 374-3319

815 Olive Street, Room 242
St. Louis, MO 63101
(314) 425-6600

Montana
Federal Office Building
301 South Park Street
Drawer 10054
Helena, MT 59626
(406) 449-5381

Nebraska
Empire State Building
Nineteenth and Farnam Streets
Omaha, NE 68102
(402) 221-4691

Nevada
301 East Stewart
P.O. Box 7527
Las Vegas, NV 89125
(702) 388-6611

New Hampshire
P.O. Box 1257
55 Pleasant Street
Room 211
Concord, NH 03301
(603) 224-4041

New Jersey
60 Park Place
Fourth Floor
Military Park Building
Newark, NJ 07102
(201) 645-3580

New Mexico
5000 Marble Avenue, N.E.
Patio Plaza Building
Suite 320
Albuquerque, NM 87110
(505) 766-3430

New York
26 Federal Plaza
Room 3100

New York, NY 10278
(212) 264-9487

100 South Clinton Street
Room 1071
Syracuse, NY 13260
(315) 423-5383

North Carolina
230 South Tryon Street
Suite 700
Charlotte, NC 28202
(704) 371-6561

North Dakota
P.O. Box 3086
653 Second Avenue North
Room 218
Fargo, ND 58108
(701) 237-5771

Ohio
AJC Federal Building
1240 East Ninth Street
Room 317
Cleveland, OH 44199
(216) 522-4180

Federal Building
U.S. Courthouse, Room 512
85 Marconi Boulevard
Columbus, OH 43215
(614) 469-6860

Oklahoma
200 Northwest Fifth Street
Federal Building, Suite 670
Oklahoma City, OK 73102
(405) 231-4301

Oregon
Federal Building, Room 676
1220 Southwest Third Ave.
Portland, OR 97204
(503) 221-2682

Pennsylvania
One Bala Cynwyd Plaza
231 St. Asaphs Road
Suite 400
East Lobby

Bala Cynwyd, PA 19004
(215) 596-5889

Convention Tower
960 Penn Avenue, 5th Floor
Pittsburgh, PA 15222
(412) 644-2780

Rhode Island
380 Westminster Mall
Fifth Floor
Providence, RI 02903
(401) 528-4580

South Carolina
1835 Assembly Street
Third Floor
P.O. Box 2786
Columbia, SC 29202
(803) 765-5373

South Dakota
Security Building, Suite 101
101 South Main Avenue
Sioux Falls, SD 57102
(605) 336-2980, ext. 231

Tennessee
Parkway Tower, Room 1012
404 James Robertson Parkway
Nashville, TN 37219
(615) 251-5881

Texas
1100 Commerce Street
Room 3C36
Dallas, TX 75242
(214) 767-0605

10737 Gateway West
Suite 320
El Paso, TX 79935
(915) 541-7678

222 East Van Buren
Suite 500
Harlingen, TX 78550
(512) 423-8934

2525 Murworth, Suite 112

Houston, TX 77054
(713) 660-4401

1611 10th Street, Suite 200
Lubbock, TX 79401
(806) 743-7462

727 East Durango
Federal Building
Room A-513
San Antonio, TX 78206
(512) 229-6250

Utah
125 South State Street
Room 2237
Salt Lake City, UT 84138
(801) 524-5800

Vermont
87 State Street, Room 205
P.O. Box 605
Montpelier, VT 05602
(802) 229-0538

Virginia
400 North Eighth Street
Room 3015
P.O. Box 10126
Federal Building
Richmond, VA 23240
(804) 771-2741

Washington
915 Second Avenue
Federal Building, Room 1792
Seattle, WA 98174
(206) 442-5534

P.O. Box 2167
651 U.S. Courthouse
920 Riverside Avenue
Spokane, WA 99210
(509) 456-3786

West Virginia
168 West Main Street
Sixth Floor
P.O. Box 1608
Clarksburg, WV 26302–1608
(304) 623-5631

231

Wisconsin
212 East Washington Avenue
Room 213
Madison, WI 53703
(608) 264-5261

Wyoming
100 East B Street
Federal Building
Room 4001
P.O. Box 2839–82602
Casper, WY 82602
(307) 261-5761

Puerto Rico/Virgin Islands
Federal Building, Room 691
Carlos Chardon Avenue
Hato Rey, PR 00918
(809) 753-4520

SBA SERVICE CORPS OF RETIRED EXECUTIVES (SCORE), National Office (202) 653-6279
CHAPTER LOCATION

Alabama
Birmingham
Foley
Mobile
Tuscaloosa

Arizona
Phoenix
Tempe
Tucson

Arkansas
Arkadelphia
Fort Smith
Little Rock

California
Arroyo Grande
Bloomington
Camarillo
Fresno
Garden Grove
Los Angeles
Pacific Palisades
Palm Springs
Pomona
Sacramento
San Diego
San Francisco
San Jose
Santa Ana
Santa Barbara
Santa Maria
Santa Rosa
Stockton

Colorado
Boulder
Colorado Springs
Craig
Denver
Durango
Fort Morgan
Glenwood Springs
Grand Junction
Lamar

Connecticut
Bridgeport
Danbury
Hartford
New Haven
Norwich
Stamford
Torrington
Waterbury
West Haven

Delaware
Wilmington

District of Columbia
Washington

Florida
Chotawatchee
Cocoa Beach
Coral Gables
Daytona Beach
Deland
Del Ray Beach
Fort Lauderdale
Fort Myers

Fort Pierce
Gainesville
Hollywood
Jacksonville
Leesburg
New Port Richey
Ocala
Orlando
Panama City
Pensacola
Punta Gorda
Sarasota
Sebring
St. Petersburg
Tallahassee
Tampa
West Palm Beach
Winter Haven
Withlacoochee

Georgia
Albany
Atlanta
Augusta
Brunswick
Gainesville
Macon
Savannah
Statesboro

Hawaii
Honolulu
Lihue, Kauai

Idaho
Blackfoot
Boise

Illinois
Aurora
Chicago
Decatur
Granite City
Marion
Moline
Peoria
Quincy

Indiana
Columbus
Evansville
Fort Wayne
Gary
Indianapolis
Kokomo
Muncie
South Bend
Terre Haute

Iowa
Burlington
Cedar Rapids
Council Bluffs
Davenport
Des Moines
Dubuque
Fort Dodge
Iowa City
Marshalltown
Mason City
Ottumwa
Sioux Falls
Spencer
Waterloo

Kansas
Belleville
Dodge City
Emporia
Garden City
Great Bend
Hays
Hutchinson
Liberal
Manhattan
Salina

Wellington
Wichita

Kentucky
Bowling Green
Covington
Lexington
Louisville
Owensboro
Paducah

Louisiana
Alexandria
Baton Rouge
Lafayette
Lake Charles
New Orleans
Shreveport
West Monroe

Maine
Augusta
Bangor
Bath
Calais
Camden
Caribou
Ellsworth
Houlton
Lewiston
Norway
Portland
Waterville

Maryland
Annapolis
Baltimore
Frostburg
Salisbury
Towson

Massachusetts
Boston
Brockton
Charleston
Fitchburg
Hyannis
New Bedford
Springfield
Worcester

Michigan
Detroit
Grand Rapids
Kalamazoo
Lansing
Menominee

Minnesota
Duluth
Mankato
Minneapolis
Rochester
St. Cloud
St. Paul

Mississippi
Biloxi
Columbus
Jackson
Meridian
Tupelo

Missouri
Branson
Camdenton
Cape Girardeau
Columbia
Hannibal
Joplin
Kansas City
Mexico
Pittsburg
Poplar Bluff
Rolla
St. Charles
St. Joseph
St. Louis
Sedalia
Sikeston
Topeka

Montana
Billings
Bozeman
Butte
Great Falls
Havre
Helena
Kalispell

Missoula
Sidney

Nebraska
Columbus
Fremont
Grand Island
Lincoln
Norfolk
North Platte
Omaha
Panhandle

Nevada
Las Vegas
Reno

New Hampshire
Concord
Keene
Laconia
Lebanon
Manchester
North Conway
Portsmouth

New Jersey
Atlantic City
Bergen County
Camden
Essex Counties
Lakewood
Monmouth County
Montclair
Newark
Somerset
Trenton

New Mexico
Albuquerque
Farmington
Las Cruces
Roswell
Santa Fe

New York
Albany
Auburn
Binghamton
Buffalo
Elmira

Hauppauge
Hornell
Huntington
Ithaca
Jamestown
Middletown
Mineola
Mt. Vernon
New York City
Ogdensburg
Poughkeepsie
Rochester
Saratoga
Staten Island
Syracuse
Utica

North Carolina
Asheville
Chapel Hill
Charlotte
Durham
Fayetteville
Gastonia
Greensboro
Greenville
Hendersonville
Hickory
High Point
Kitty Hawk
Raleigh
Southern Pines
Wilmington

North Dakota
Bismarck
Devil's Lake
Dickinson
Fargo
Grand Forks
Jamestown
Mandan
Minot
Williston

Ohio
Akron
Cincinnati
Cleveland

Columbus
Dayton
Hocking Valley
Lima
Mansfield
Marietta
Newark
New Philadelphia
Springfield
Steubenville
Toledo
Youngstown

Oklahoma
Enid
Lawton
Oklahoma City
Tulsa

Oregon
Bend
Medford-Talent
Portland
Salem
Williamette

Pennsylvania
Bala Cynwyd
Bethlehem
Erie
Greensburg
Harrisburg
Lancaster
Monessen
Pittsburgh
Reading
Scranton
Uniontown
Wilkes-Barre
Williams Port
Yorktown

Puerto Rico
Hato Rey
Mayaguez Playa

Rhode Island
Providence

South Carolina
Charleston
Columbia

Florence
Greenville

South Dakota
Aberdeen
Pierre
Rapid City
Sioux Falls

Tennessee
Chattanooga
Greeneville
Jackson
Knoxville
Memphis
Morristown
Nashville

Texas
Abilene
Amarillo
Austin
Brazoport
Brownsville
College Station
Corpus Christi
Dallas
El Paso
Fort Worth
Galveston
Houston
Longview
Lower Rio Grande

Lubbock
Mount Pleasant
Odessa
San Angelo
San Antonio
Tyler
Waco
Wichita Falls

Utah
Ogden
Provo
Salt Lake City

Vermont
Brattleboro
Burlington
Montpelier
Rutland

Virginia
Bristol
Charlottesville
Danville
Hampton
Norfolk
Norton
Richmond
Richlands
Roanoke
Suffolk
Waynesboro
Winchester
Wise

Virgin Islands
St. Thomas

Washington
Bellingham
Everett
Seattle
Spokane
Tacoma

West Virginia
Charleston
Clarksburg
Elkins
Jackson
Marshall
Parkersburg
Princeton
Wheeling

Wisconsin
Appleton
Eau Claire
La Crosse
Madison
Milwaukee
Rhinelander
Shell Lake
Wausau

Wyoming
Casper
Cheyenne
Sheridan

Index

Absenteeism, 110–111
Accountant, hiring an, 178–179
Active Corp of Executives (ACE), 74
Adler, Fred, 82
Almanac of Business and Industrial Financial Ratios, The, 123
Annual Statement Studies, 123
Assistance, obtaining, 74–76
Associations, professional/trade, 75–76, 142–143

Bardwick, Judith, 12, 13
Better Business Bureau, 135
Birch, David, 26
Burch, John G., 28
Business Failure Record, 8
Business Package, 60
Business Planning Guide, 60
Business plans, developing
  example outline for, 38–45
  information on preparing, 60
  purpose of, 35–36
  SBA's example of, 45–59

237

Sheldon's laws, 36
updating of, 59–60
Business start-ups
definition of, 10
effort needed for, 16–17
reasons for, 12–14
statistics on, 6–7

Cahners Publishing Company, 119
Cash flow planning, 83–87
Chamber of Commerce, 75, 135
Checklist for Going Into Business for Yourself, 17
Clients, choosing, 205–206
Collection
checklist for, 170–171
credit checks and, 164–165
examples of problems with, 160–161, 163–164
problems for the entrepreneur, 161–162
stages of, 165–170
Computers
choosing a vendor, 134–137
defining your needs, 131–132
erasing information, 129–130
how to buy, 130–131
software, 132–134
Consultant, hiring a, 74, 179–184
Contracts
bidding on estimations, 201–202
bidding on unreliable descriptions or specifications, 200–201
bidding under deadlines, 202–203
creative/exploratory procurements, 203–204
number of contracts to bid on, 209–210
overoptimism about, 199–200

reading all parts of the, 198–199
resolving disputes, 204–205
unrealistic time frames, 203
Coopers and Lybrand, 63
Corporate world, reentering the, 211–222
Cost of Doing Business, 123
Credit checks, 164–165
Credit rating, 87–90
Cummingham, Robert S., 144

Drucker, Peter, 185
Dun & Bradstreet Corporation (D&B), 8–11, 19, 20–23, 123, 135

Earnings, low personal, 93–94
Employee Retirement Income Security Act of 1974 (ERISA), 65
Employee theft, 111–113
Encyclopedia of Associations, 75
Entrepreneur(s)
adaptability of, 17–18
assessing your potential as, 31–33
characteristics needed by, 28–30
common weaknesses of, 30–31
decision–making ability of, 17
definition of an, 27–28
knowledge needed by, 18
life style of, 14–15, 17
Entrepreneurship, 28
Entrepreneurship and Small Business Management, 60
Expenses
energy, 118–119
equipment, 119–120
example of overlooked, 37–38
failure and, 19–20
goods sold and, 116–118